GUIDE TO
KOREAN CULTURAL HERITAGE

GUIDE TO
KOREAN CULTURAL HERITAGE

HOLLYM
Elizabeth, NJ · Seoul

GUIDE TO KOREAN CULTURAL HERITAGE

Copyright © 1995, 2003
by Korean Overseas Information Service

Originally published in 1995
by Korean Overseas Information Service

Revised edition, 2003
Second printing, 2004
by Hollym International Corp.
18 Donald Place, Elizabeth, NJ 07208, U.S.A.
Phone: (908)353-1655   Fax: (908)353-0255
http://www.hollym.com

Published simultaneously in Korea
by Hollym Corporation; Publishers
13-13 Gwancheol-dong, Jongno-gu, Seoul 110-111, Korea
Phone (82 2)735-7551~4   Fax: (82 2)730-5149, 8192
http://www.hollym.co.kr   e-mail: info@hollym.co.kr

ISBN: 1-56591-213-6

Printed in Korea

Preface

Koreans take great pride in their cultural heritage for ample reason. The ancient kingdoms of Goguryeo, Baekje and Silla (1st century B.C.-A.D. 7th century) produced some of the world's most outstanding Buddhist arts. Goryeo, the dynasty that ruled Korea from 918 to 1392, produced inlaid celadon ceramics of unexcelled beauty and the *Tripitaka Koreana*, the world's most comprehensive compilation of Buddhist scriptures, and some 80,000 woodblocks to print it. It also developed the world's first movable metal printing type, some 200 years before it was developed in the West.

Joseon, which ruled Korea from 1392 to 1910, invented the world's first rain gauge in 1441 and ironclad battleship as well as one of the most scientific writing systems in the world.

Seven of Korea's most prized cultural assets are included on the World Cultural Heritage List of the United Nations Educational, Scientific and Cultural Organization (UNESCO). They are Bulguksa Temple and Seokguram Grotto; the woodblocks of the *Tripitaka Koreana* and their storage halls at Haeinsa Temple; Jongmyo, the royal ancestral shrine of the Joseon Dynasty; Changdeokgung Palace, the Hwaseong Fortress in Suwon; Gyeongju Historic Sites; and Gochang, Hwasun and Ganghwa Dolmen Sites. In addition, *Hunminjeongeum*, the explication issued when King Sejong promulgated the Korean alphabet, Hangeul, in 1446, and the *Joseonwangjosillok (The Veritable Records of the Joseon Dynasty)* are included on UNESCO's Memory of the World List.

In an effort to make Korean culture better known around the world, ten symbols have been chosen. They will be used in much the same way a company uses symbols to promote its corporate identity (CI). They are *hanbok*, Korea's national costume; *kimchi* and *bulgogi*, spicy fermented vegetables and grilled marinated meat; *Hangeul*, the Korean alphabet; *jeryeak*, the music of the Jongmyo ancestral rites; *talchum*, masked dance drama; *taekwondo*, a Korean martial art; Korean ginseng; Bulguksa and Seokguram; Mt. Seoraksan, and some world-renowned artists of Korean origin.

The ten symbols, or cultural images, are introduced in this volume along with 15 other aspects of Korean culture ranging from rites of passage and other customs, traditional sports and gardening to various handicrafts, printing, painting, and pottery to give the reader a glimpse of Korea's rich cultural heritage.

Contents

A Guide to
Korean Cultural Heritage

Hanbok
Korean Dress

A walk down almost any street in Korea will reveal that today's Korean wardrobe ranges from jeans and rock fashions to tailored suits and chic designer creations. However, of all the outfits one is likely to see, the most striking is without a doubt the *hanbok*, the traditional costume worn by Koreans of all ages, particularly on traditional holidays and when attending social affairs with a Korean overtone.

The hanbok is characterized by simple lines and no pockets. The women's *hanbok* comprises a wrap-around skirt and a bolero-like jacket. It is often called *chima-jeogori, chima* being the Korean word for skirt and *jeogori* the word for jacket. The men's *hanbok* consists of a short jacket and pants, called *baji*, that are roomy and bound at the ankles. Both ensembles may be topped by a long coat of a similar cut called *durumagi*.

The traditional-style *hanbok* worn today are patterned after the ones worn during the Confucian-oriented Joseon Dynasty (1392-1910). *Yangban*, a hereditary aristocratic class based on

The attire worn by high-ranking Joseon Dynasty (1392-1910) official and his wife for national holidays such as New Year's Day.

Commoners were also allowed to wear the formal clothes on their wedding day.

scholarship and official position rather than on wealth, wore brightly colored *hanbok* of plain and patterned silk in cold weather and of closely woven ramie cloth or other high-grade, light-weight materials in warm weather. Commoners, on the other hand, were restricted by law as well as finances to bleached hemp and cotton and could only wear white and sometimes pale pink, light green, gray and charcoal.

Young women wore red *chima* and yellow *jeogori* prior to marriage and red *chima* and green *jeogori* after the wedding when bowing to their parents-in-law and when paying respect to them upon returning from the honeymoon. Today,

however, women usually wear pink *hanbok* for engagement ceremonies, Western-style wedding dresses and the traditional red skirt and green jacket after the wedding when greeting their in-laws after the honeymoon. On other occasions, they wear *hanbok* of almost any color and fabric including embroidered, hand-painted, or gold-stamped silk, but white is worn mostly by old people and used for mourning clothes.

Yangban women wore wrap-around skirts 12 *pok* (a width of cloth) wide and lapped them on the left side whereas commoners were prohibited from wearing *chima* of more than 10 or 11 *pok* and were required to wrap them on the right. Under the *hanbok*, women generally wore, and most still do, a pair of long bloomers, a long, one-piece slip worn somewhat like a high-waisted, one-piece dress, and a jacket-like piece a little smaller than

the *jeogori*. The fullness of the *chima* allows the wearing of any number of undergarments, a big plus given Korea's cold winters, and makes it wearable during pregnancy.

Nowadays skirts of two and a half widths of cloth are generally worn; however, today's cloth is about twice as wide as in ancient times. Most of today's *chima* have shoulder straps for ease in wearing. For proper appearance the *chima* should be pulled tight so that it presses the breasts flat and the slit should be just under the shoulder blade. The left side of the *chima* should be held when walking to keep it from flapping open and revealing the undergarments. Old women often hold the left side up beside the left breast.

Most *jeogori* have a snap or small tie ribbons on the inside to hold it closed. The long ribbons of the jacket are tied to form the *otgoreum*, a bow that is different from the butterfly-like bow of the

The queen's outer robe and accessories, including hair ornaments, pendants and shoes.

West. The *otgoreum* is very important for it is one of three things by which the beauty and quality of a *hanbok* is judged. The other two are the curve of the sleeves and the way the *git*, a band of fabric that trims the collar and front of the *jeogori*, is terminated. The ends of the *git* are generally squared off. A removable white collar called *dongjeong* is basted over the *git*.

As the *hanbok* have no pockets, women and men both carried all types of purses, or *jumeoni*. These were basically of two major types: a round one and a pleated, somewhat triangular one, both closed with a drawstring. These were embellished with elaborate knots and tassels that varied according to the status and gender of the bearer.

Although some of the basic elements of today's *hanbok* and its accessories were probably worn at a very

Various types of purses.

A coat-like shawl worn by a Joseon woman to cover her face when she went outside (left); a fully dressed woman (right).

early date, the two-piece costume of today did not begin to evolve until the Three Kingdoms period (57 B.C.-A.D. 668), when the kingdoms of Goguryeo, Baekje and Silla dominated the Korean Peninsula. This is clearly evident in the paintings that adorn the walls of fourth to sixth century Goguryeo tombs. The murals feature men and women dressed in long, narrow-sleeved jackets with the left side lapped over the right, trousers and boot-like footwear. Such garments were probably inspired by the harsh northern climate and terrain and a nomadic lifestyle centered on horse riding. Also, owing to geopolitical factors, it is likely that they were influenced by Chinese styles of dress. Baekje and Silla had similar costumes.

Silk mandarin robes introduced from

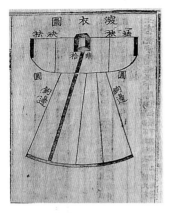

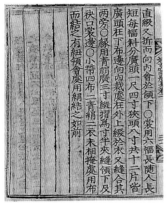

An illustrated instruction on how to make a dress, published in 1827.

neighboring Tang China were adopted for wear by royalty and officials in 648 by Silla, the kingdom that eventually unified the peninsula in 668. The robes were worn over the native costume. Noble women began to wear full-length skirt-trousers and wide-sleeved, hip-length jackets belted at the waist, and noblemen, roomy trousers bound in at the ankles and a narrower, tunic-style jacket cuffed at the wrist and belted at the waist.

In 935, Silla was replaced by a new dynasty called Goryeo, from which the name "Korea" is derived. Buddhism, which Silla had already made the national religion, flourished along with printing and the arts, especially celadon ceramics. During the Goryeo Dynasty, the *chima* was shortened and it was hiked up above the waist and tied at the chest with a long, wide ribbon, which has remained the fashion ever since. The *jeogori* was also shortened and its sleeves were curved slightly. At the same time, women began to wear their hair in plaits on top of their heads and men began shaving their heads except for a patch in the middle.

In 1392, the Joseon Dynasty replaced Goryeo. It was founded by an ex-Goryeo general named Yi

Seonggye and his descendants ruled Korea for over 500 years. The early Joseon Dynasty kings made Neo-Confucianism the ruling ideology and, with its emphasis on formality and etiquette, dictated the style of dress for the royal family and all the members of the court as well as for aristocrats and commoners for all types of occasions including weddings and funerals. Integrity in men and chastity in women became the foremost social values and was reflected in the way people dressed. Men's *hanbok* changed very little but women's underwent many changes over the centuries.

In the 15th century, women began to wear full, pleated skirts that completely concealed the lines

New styles of hanbok designed for modern living.

Two *gisaeng* (female hostess and companion, skilled in social graces, song and dance) going for a picnic in the spring. (previous page).

of the body and long *jeogori*. With time, however, the *jeogori* was gradually shortened until it just covered the breasts, making it necessary to reduce the fullness of the *chima* so that it could be extended almost to the armpits and this remains the fashion today.

Today's designers are increasingly seeking inspiration in the *hanbok* and other costumes of their ancestors to create fashions with a uniquely Korean flair that can meet the demands of today's lifestyles. They are incorporating the lines and cut

A woman's
summer dress

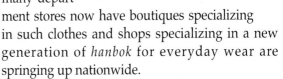

of the *hanbok* and other ancient clothes and accessories in their designs and employing traditional fabrics such as hemp and ramie. In fact, many department-ment stores now have boutiques specializing in such clothes and shops specializing in a new generation of *hanbok* for everyday wear are springing up nationwide.

Without a doubt, the *hanbok*, with roots stretching back many centuries, and designs it inspires will continue to grace the streets of Korea for many years to come.

Weaving cloth (left)
and rolls of dyed cloth (above).

Kimchi and Bulgogi

Two Healthy Korean Foods

T wo foods that people have come to identify with Korea are *kimchi*, a fermented vegetable dish, and *bulgogi*, a marinated meat dish. Whereas *kimchi* is a staple dish that is eaten at every meal, *bulgogi* is more like a party food in that it is generally eaten on special occasions and when dining out or entertaining guests. Koreans tend to favor beef when entertaining or eating out, and *bulgogi* is one of the most popular beef dishes and one that even non-Koreans find very tasty.

The word *bulgogi* is commonly translated as Korean barbecue, though it literally means "fire meat" as *bul* is "fire" or *gogi* is "meat". Beef is most often identified with *bulgogi*, but even pork, chicken, lamb, squid and octopus, for example, can be cooked *bulgogi* style as *bulgogi*, like barbecue, is a method of cooking.

For the most common beef *bulgogi*, thin slices of

Rows of Chinese cabbage ready to be picked for *kimchi*.

meat, usually tenderloin, are marinated in a sauce made of soy sauce, sesame oil, minced garlic, sesame seeds and other seasonings, and then cooked over a charcoal grill, usually at the table. The grilled beef slices can be eaten as are or wrapped in a lettuce leaf along with slices of fresh garlic and green pepper and a dab of soybean paste, red pepper paste, or a mixture of the two, all of which are rich in vitamins, minerals and cancer-fighting substances.

In some restaurants, *bulgogi* is cooked on a dome-shaped *pan* that is placed over a charcoal brazier or a gas range. The *pan* has a trough around the edge to catch the tasty juice that cooks out of the meat so that it can be eaten with one's

Marinated beef slices are cooked right at the dining table.

Other ingredients for cooking *bulgogi*, in addition to beef.

rice. *Bulgogi* can also be cooked in a regular frying pan or on an electric skillet but most connoisseurs prefer the traditional charcoal fire.

For pork and other types of *bulgogi*, a little red pepper paste is usually added to the marinade. This gives the *bulgogi* a spicy taste and aroma.

Recently, people have been finding that *bulgogi* is not only tasty and healthy but also very versatile. It has been adapted to today's fast foods with some sandwich chains adding *bulgogi* burgers to their menus and a number of well-known pizza restaurants even adopting it as one of their pizza toppings. *Bulgogi* is an ideal picnic food and, with some slight changes in the thickness and size of the meat pieces, it can become a tasty hors d'oeuvre or buffet item.

Kimchi is a pungent, fermented dish generally consisting of cabbage or turnip seasoned with salt, garlic, green onions, ginger, red pepper and shellfish. It is low in calories and cholesterol and very high in fiber. It is also very nutritious. In fact, it is richer in vitamins than apples. Had the coiner of the well-known saying "An apple a day keeps the doctor away" been Korean, perhaps he would have said "Some *kimchi* a day keeps the doctor away."

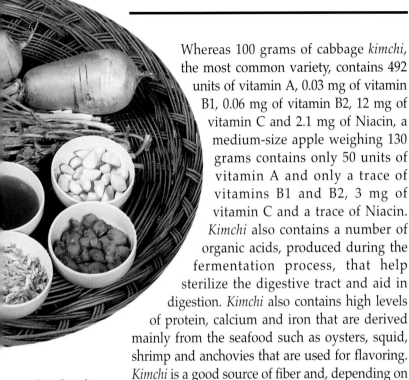

Ingredients for *kimchi*.

Whereas 100 grams of cabbage *kimchi*, the most common variety, contains 492 units of vitamin A, 0.03 mg of vitamin B1, 0.06 mg of vitamin B2, 12 mg of vitamin C and 2.1 mg of Niacin, a medium-size apple weighing 130 grams contains only 50 units of vitamin A and only a trace of vitamins B1 and B2, 3 mg of vitamin C and a trace of Niacin. *Kimchi* also contains a number of organic acids, produced during the fermentation process, that help sterilize the digestive tract and aid in digestion. *Kimchi* also contains high levels of protein, calcium and iron that are derived mainly from the seafood such as oysters, squid, shrimp and anchovies that are used for flavoring. *Kimchi* is a good source of fiber and, depending on the ingredients, may contain many of the nutrients and naturally occurring chemicals that can help combat cancers of the mouth, throat, lungs, stomach, bladder, colon and cervix.

Chinese cabbage, the main ingredient in the most commonly eaten *kimchi*, has a higher protein content than many other vegetables and a significant amount of minerals and vitamin C and its green leaves are rich in vitamin A. Radish roots, another major ingredient, are not only rich in vitamins but also diastase, an enzyme that promotes the digestion of carbohydrates. The radish stalks and leaves are also a good source of calcium, vitamin C and carotene. Green onions, a must in almost every *kimchi* recipe because of their taste and flavor, are a good source of vitamins and minerals, especially calcium. Watercress, which is also rich in calcium and vitamins A and C, is also used in most recipes for its rich flavor and aroma. Indian mustard leaves, which are also widely used because of their aroma, are rich in minerals, especially calcium and iron, and in vitamins A and C. Sponge seaweed, which is known to be helpful in preventing heart disease, is another common ingredient that produces a cool, crispy taste. It is especially rich in calcium and iodine and has a unique aroma.

Garlic, which is eaten in many ways including raw, is an essential *kimchi* ingredient as well as a mainstay of the Korean diet. It even figures in the national foundation myth. Dangun, who, according to legend, founded the Korean nation in 2333 B.C., was born of the union of a heavenly god, Hwanung, the son of the God of All and ruler of Heaven, and a bear who became a woman after eating 20 cloves of garlic and a bundle of mugwort and staying out of the sunlight for 21 days. Recent studies show that garlic may help prevent stomach cancer and reduce blood cholesterol levels.

It is the red chili peppers, however, that make *kimchi* a truly remarkable health food and different from the *ju* and *osinko* of China and Japan that are often likened to *kimchi* but are

The process of making *kimchi*.
1. Chinese cabbage is sliced and washed and then put into salt water.
2, 3. Spices and thinly sliced vegetables such as green onions are prepared.
4. The thinly sliced vegetables and spices are mixed.
5, 6. The spiced vegetables are inserted into the cabbage leaves to make *kimchi*.

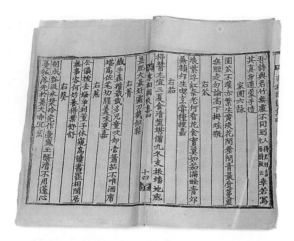

The *Donggukisanggukjip* (The Collected Works of Minister Yi Gyubo), published in 1251, describes *kimchi*.

basically nothing more than Chinese cabbage or radish pickled in salt. Chili peppers not only give *kimchi* its distinctive spicy flavor and appetizing color but also contain an element called capsicin that prevents the taste of *kimchi* from turning by checking the decomposition process. It also checks the acidifying process to which vitamin C is exceptionally vulnerable and keeps the vegetables fresh so that the eater experiences the sensation of biting into crispy fresh vegetables. Capsicin also has another remarkable property that is only activated in *kimchi*; it can break down fats in the body. These properties and the large doses of vitamins A, B and C make peppers truly remarkable.

But chili peppers have not always been a major ingredient in *kimchi*. Koreans did not know the chili pepper until the late 16th century or early 17th century when Portuguese traders based in

Each region and each family has its own unique varieties of *kimchi*.

Baechu kimchi

Kkakdugi

Chonggak kimchi

Oisobagi

Nabak kimchi made
on Jejudo island

Pyeongyang-style
baechu kimchi

Nagasaki, Japan, who, having brought it from Central America, introduced it to the country.

Early historical records of *kimchi* making do not mention red peppers or garlic. Various spellings of the dish appear but they all share the same meaning: vegetables soaked in salt water. One of the earliest, if not the earliest, descriptions of *kimchi* making is in a work by Yi Gyubo (1168-1241), a noted literary figure during the Goryeo Dynasty (918-1392), in which he describes the preparation of turnips for storing for food for winter. A more detailed description of *kimchi* appears in a recipe book written in the late 1600s but the first mention of *kimchi* seasoned with red pepper is in a cookbook printed in 1765. Recipes closely resembling today's *kimchi* appear in two cookbooks published in the early 1800s.

Regardless of when red pepper was added to *kimchi*, it was an epochal event. The addition of red peppers not only enhanced the taste of the otherwise salty vegetables and kept them crunchy like fresh ones but also turned *kimchi* into a healthful, vitamin-packed food that can play a vital role in preventing disease. Of course, over the years *kimchi* has become even more nutritional with the addition of more and more ingredients such as carrots, pears, chestnuts, pine nuts, abalone, seaweed and the ones previously mentioned.

There are basically two kinds of *kimchi*, seasonal and winter, with numerous varieties of each. The seasonal varieties are made with

Kimchi is stored and fermented in crocks. (previous page)

A drawing of a section of a palace showing rows of crocks that stored *kimchi*.

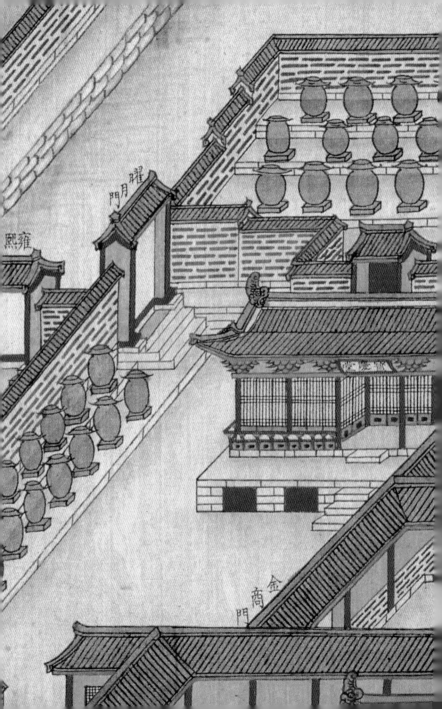

雍熙

曜月門

金商門

In order to control the temperature of *kimchi* throughout the winter, a crock containing *kimchi* is buried in the ground.

whatever vegetables are available and are for short-term storage. The winter varieties, made with mostly cabbages and turnips, are for long-term storage to provide vegetables during the cold winter months.

Baechu kimchi is the most prevalent type. To make it, Chinese cabbages *(baechu)* are first trimmed, split down the middle and put in brine to soak. When they are soft, they are rinsed in cold water and drained. Meanwhile, julienne cut radish strips are mixed with a red pepper paste made of red pepper powder and water. To this are added crushed garlic, salt, thinly sliced green onions, and a variety of other seasonings, depending on the region and the cook's budget, to make a stuffing. The stuffing is packed between the layers of cabbage leaves and each cabbage is wrapped with a few leaves. Finally, the cabbages are stacked in a crock, jar or other appropriate container, covered with salted cabbage leaves, pressed down firmly and covered.

The storage temperature of the *gimjang kimchi*, as winter *kimchi* is called, should be well controlled throughout the winter to prevent over fermentation and thus souring. The traditional way of doing this is to bury the crocks of *kimchi* in the ground but, because this is not always possible for urbanites, specially designed containers have come into use in recent years.

Winter *kimchi* is usually made in late November and early December when the weather is quite nippy. At the time, women gather in groups throughout the country to turn mountains of cabbages and turnips into *kimchi* to feed their families throughout the cold winter months.

However, *kimchi* is not made in as great quantities as it used to be. Today an urban family of five will make 20 to 30 cabbages into winter *kimchi* whereas in the past it would have made between 70 and 100. The decline in home production is due to several factors: hot house vegetables are available year-round; apartment living makes large-scale production unfeasible; and, factory-made *kimchi* can be purchased in supermarkets as there are now many companies that produce it for local consumption as well as for export.

In addition to being eaten as a staple side dish,

kimchi is also used in a variety of cooked dishes. The most common is *kimchi jjigae*, a hot, fiery stew made by boiling *kimchi* with pork. *Kimchi* is also stir-fried with thin strips of pork and eaten with fresh tofu, or *dubu* as bean curd is known in Korean. It is also dipped in a flour-based batter and fried.

To most Koreans, a meal without *kimchi*, no matter how lavish, is incomplete or even unthinkable. It spikes the rice, titillates the taste buds, and, perhaps, keeps the doctor away. It is an ideal health food as well as diet food and with its increasing inclusion on supermarket shelves around the world and its designation as an official food at events such as the 1998 World Cup in France, it is fast becoming an international food to be enjoyed around the world.

Women preparing Chinese cabbage in the initial stage of *kimchi* making.

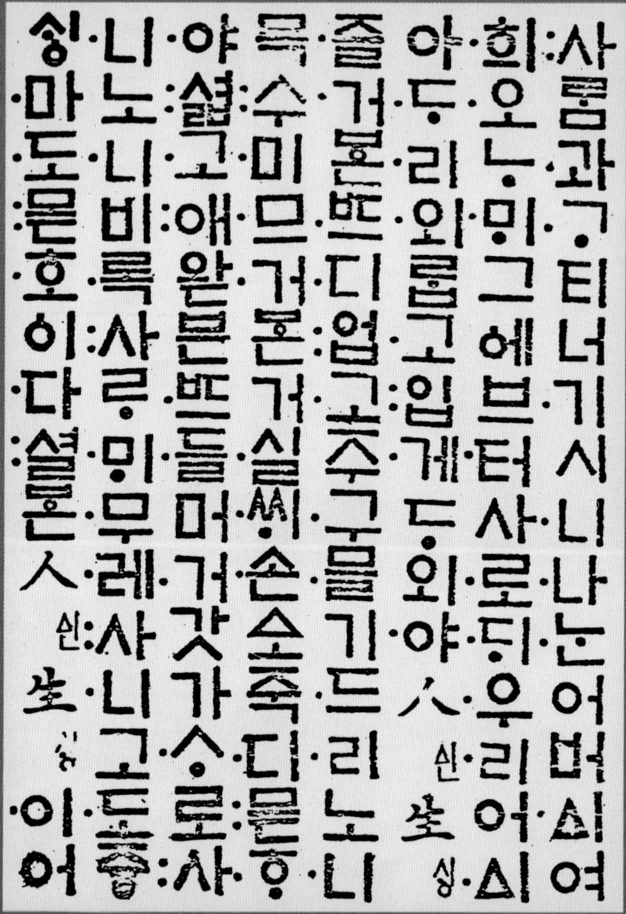

The term *Hangeul* refers to the Korean alphabet.
Shown here is *Seokbosangjeol* to which the origin of
Hangeul can be traced. Early Joseon period.

Hangeul

The Korean Alphabet

Koreans have developed and use a unique alphabet called *Hangeul*. It is considered to be one of the most efficient alphabets in the world and has garnered unanimous praise from language experts for its scientific design and excellence.

Hangeul was created under King Sejong during the Joseon Dynasty (1392-1910). In 1446, the first Korean alphabet was proclaimed under the name *Hunminjeongeum*, which literally meant "the Correct Sounds for the Instruction of the People."

King Sejong, the motivating force behind *Hangeul* , is considered to be one of the greatest rulers in the history of Korea. Highly respected for his benevolent disposition and diligence, King Sejong was also a passionate scholar whose knowledge and natural talent in all fields of study astounded even the most learned experts.

When King Sejong was not performing his official duties, he enjoyed reading and meditating. He could also be very tenacious at times and would never yield on what he thought was right. Love for the people was the

나 랏 말 ᄊ ᆞ미 中듀ᇰ國귁에 달아 文문字ᄍᆞ와로 서르 ᄉᆞᄆᆞᆺ디 아니ᄒᆞᆯᄊ ᆡ이런 젼ᄎᆞ로 어린 百ᄇᆡ᠎ᆨ姓셔ᇰ이 니르고져 호ᇙ배 이셔도 ᄆᆞᄎᆞᆷ내 제ᄠᅳ들 시러 펴디 몯ᄒ ᆞᇙ노미 하니라 내 이ᄅᆞᆯ為윙ᄒ ᆞ야 어엿비 너겨 새로 스믈 여듧 字ᄍ ᆞᄅᆞᆯ ᄆᆡᇰᄀᆞ노니 사ᄅᆞᆷ마다 ᄒ ᆡᅇᅧ수ᄫᅵ니겨 날로 ᄡ ᅮ메 便뼌安한킈 ᄒᆞ고져 ᄒ ᆞᇙᄯᆞᄅᆞ미니라

cornerstone of his reign(1418-1450), and he was always ready to listen to the voices of the common folk. He was a ruler of virtue, with the welfare of the people dictating all policy formulations.

King Sejong also established the *Jiphyeonjeon*, an academic research institute, inside the palace. Noted scholars from all academic disciplines gathered here to engage in lively discussions and also to publish a variety of quality books.

During his reign, King Sejong always deplored the fact that the common people, ignorant of the complicated Chinese characters that were being used by the educated, were not able to read and write. He understood their frustration in not being able to read or to communicate their thoughts and feelings in written words.

The Chinese script was used by the intelligentsia of the country, but being of foreign origin, it could not fully express the words and meaning of Korean thoughts and spoken language. Therefore, common people with

The book *Hunminjeongeum haerye* uses five explanations and one example to explain *Hangeul* (right).

Hangeul, created under King Sejong, was first proclaimed as *Hunminjeongeum*.

legitimate complaints had no way of submitting their grievances to the appropriate authorities, other than through oral communication, and they had no way to record for posterity the agricultural wisdom and knowledge they had gained through years of experience.

King Sejong felt great sympathy for the people. As a wise ruler strongly dedicated to national identity and cultural independence, he immediately searched for solutions. What he envisioned was an alphabet that was uniquely Korean and easily learnable, rendering it accessible and usable for the common people.

Thus, the *Hunminjeongeum* was born. In the preface of its proclamation, King Sejong states as follows:

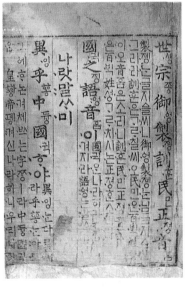

"Being of foreign origin, Chinese characters are incapable of capturing uniquely Korean meanings. Therefore, many common people have no way to express their thoughts and feelings. Out of my sympathy for their difficulties, I have invented a set of 28 letters. The letters are very easy to learn, and it is my fervent hope that they improve the quality of life of all people." The statement captures the essence of King Sejong's determination and dedication to cultural independence and

commitment to the welfare of the people.

When first proclaimed by King Sejong, *Hunminjeongeum* had 28 letters in all, of which only 24 are in use today. The 24 letters are as follows.

Consonants: ㄱ(g,k), ㄴ (n), ㄷ (d, t), ㄹ (r , l),
　　　　　ㅁ(m), ㅂ (b, p), ㅅ (s), ㅇ (voiceless),
　　　　　ㅈ (j), ㅊ (ch), ㅋ (k), ㅌ (t), ㅍ (p), ㅎ (h)

Vowels: ㅏ (a), ㅑ (ya), ㅓ (eo), ㅕ (yeo),
　　　　ㅗ (o), ㅛ (yo), ㅜ (u), ㅠ (yu), ㅡ (eu), ㅣ (i)

The basic letters of the alphabet when *Hunminjeongeum* was first created numbered eight; they were the consonants "ㄱ, ㄴ, ㅁ, ㅅ, ㅇ" and the vowels "•, ㅡ, ㅣ"

The reason consonants and vowels were separated was due to their differing functions when two letters were combined to form a syllable. *Hunminjeongeum* is basically a form of hieroglyph. Consonants, the initial sound letters, resemble a person's speech organs. The shape of each letter is based on the form of different sound articulation units.

"ㄱ (giyeok)": To pronounce this letter, part of the tongue touches the molar teeth and sticks near the uvula. The shape of the letter is based on the lateral form of this process.

"ㄴ (nieun)": To pronounce this letter, the front of the tongue curves and the tip of the tongue sticks to the upper gums. The shape of the letter is based on the lateral form of this

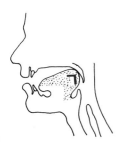

Root of the letter " ㄱ "(g,k). Back of the tongue sticks near the uvula.

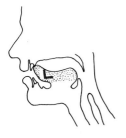

Root of the letter "ㄴ "(n). The tip of the tongue sticks to the upper gums.

A portrait of King Sejong, the leading force behind the creation of Korea's own alphabet, *Hunminjeongeum* (left).

process.

"ㅁ (mieum)": To pronounce this letter, the upper and lower lips are joined. The shape of the letter is based on the form of the joined lips.

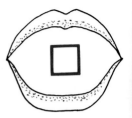

Root of the letter "ㅁ" (m). Joined lips.

"ㅅ (siot)": To pronounce this letter, the tip of the tongue and the upper teeth are brought close together, and sound is created by blowing through the narrowed passage. The shape of the letter is based on the form of the teeth during the process.

"ㅇ (ieung)": To pronounce this letter that is created by stimulating the uvula, the throat assumes a round shape, hence the form of the consonant.

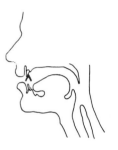

Root of the letter "ㅅ" (s). Sharp teeth.

Nine additional letters were made by adding additional strokes to the five basic consonants based on the strength of the sounds, as follows.

ㄱ - ㅋ
ㄴ - ㄷ, ㅌ
ㅁ - ㅂ, ㅍ
ㅅ - ㅈ, ㅊ
ㅇ - ㆆ, ㅎ

However, "ㆆ" is no longer used.

The vowels, on the other hand, were created in the image of the sky, land, and man. That is '•' resembles the roundness of the sky, '—' represents the flat land and 'ㅣ' is the image of a standing man. The other vowels "ㅏ, ㅑ, ㅓ, ㅕ, ㅗ, ㅛ, ㅜ, ㅠ" are variations of these three basic vowels.

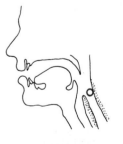

Root of the letter "ㅇ" (voiceless). Round-shaped throat.

The creation of the *Hunminjeongeum* was a remarkable accomplishment. Creating consonants based on a person's speech organs and vowels based on the shapes of the sky, land, and man was truly a revolutionary and unprecedented process.

King Sejong and the scholars of the *Jiphyeonjeon*, inventors of the Korean alphabet, considered human sounds as being more than mere physical phenomena. They assumed that an invisible yet more powerful principle was the controlling force behind these phenomena. They

Yeongbi (right) and a rubbed copy (left). This is the oldest stone monument written in *Hangeul* and was used when *Hunminjeongeum* was created.

adhered to the principle that human sounds and all universal phenomena are based on *eum-yang* (negative-positive) and *ohaeng* (the five primary elements: metal, wood, water, fire and earth). Hence, they thought it natural that there be a common link between sounds and the changing of the seasons and between sounds and music.

A Korean syllable is divided into three parts: *choseong* (initial consonant), *jungseong* (vowel), and *jongseong* (final consonant). This is the basic framework that King Sejong and the *Jiphyeonjeon* scholars adhered to when creating the letters. *Jongseong* was not separately created and was a repetition of the *choseong*. Therefore, *Hangeul* is

The Story of Hong Gildong, a work of fiction written in *Hangeul* the Korean alphabet.

The Korean alphabet

Vowels Consonants	ㅏ (a)	ㅑ (ya)	ㅓ (eo)	ㅕ (yeo)	ㅗ (o)	ㅛ (yo)	ㅜ (u)	ㅠ (yu)	ㅡ (eu)	ㅣ (i)
ㄱ (g, k)	가	갸	거	겨	고	교	구	규	그	기
ㄴ (n)	나	냐	너	녀	노	뇨	누	뉴	느	니
ㄷ (d, t)	다	댜	더	뎌	도	됴	두	듀	드	디
ㄹ (r, l)	라	랴	러	려	로	료	루	류	르	리
ㅁ (m)	마	먀	머	며	모	묘	무	뮤	므	미
ㅂ (b, p)	바	뱌	버	벼	보	뵤	부	뷰	브	비
ㅅ (s)	사	샤	서	셔	소	쇼	수	슈	스	시
ㅇ (ng)	아	야	어	여	오	요	우	유	으	이
ㅈ (j)	자	쟈	저	져	조	죠	주	쥬	즈	지
ㅊ (ch)	차	챠	처	쳐	초	쵸	추	츄	츠	치
ㅋ (k)	카	캬	커	켜	코	쿄	쿠	큐	크	키
ㅌ (t)	타	탸	터	텨	토	툐	투	튜	트	티
ㅍ (p)	파	퍄	퍼	펴	포	표	푸	퓨	프	피
ㅎ (h)	하	햐	허	혀	호	효	후	휴	흐	히

The first copy of Korea's first privately-owned newspaper, the *Dongnipsinmum* (The Independent). Launched on April 7, 1896, the paper was the country's first to use only *Hangeul*.

capable of creating thousands of words by combining the consonants and vowels.

ㄱ+ㅏ=가 (ga)   ㄴ+ㅏ=나 (na)   ㄷ+ㅏ=다 (da)   ㄹ+ㅏ=라 (ra)

ㄱ+ㅑ=갸 (gya)   ㄴ+ㅑ=냐 (nya)   ㄷ+ㅑ=댜 (dya)   ㄹ+ㅑ=랴 (rya)

ㄱ+ㅓ=거 (geo)   ㄴ+ㅓ=너 (neo)   ㄷ+ㅓ=더 (deo)   ㄹ+ㅓ=러 (reo)

ㄱ+ㅕ=겨 (gyeo)ㄴ+ㅕ=녀 (nyeo)   ㄷ+ㅕ=뎌 (dyeo)   ㄹ+ㅕ=려 (ryeo)

ㄱ+ㅗ=고 (go)   ㄴ+ㅗ=노 (no)   ㄷ+ㅗ=도 (do)   ㄹ+ㅗ=로 (ro)

ㄱ+ㅛ=교 (gyo)   ㄴ+ㅛ=뇨 (nyo)   ㄷ+ㅛ=됴 (dyo)   ㄹ+ㅛ=료 (ryo)

ㄱ+ㅜ=구 (gu)   ㄴ+ㅜ=누 (nu)   ㄷ+ㅜ=두 (du)   ㄹ+ㅜ=루 (ru)

ㄱ+ㅠ=규 (gyu)   ㄴ+ㅠ=뉴 (nyu)   ㄷ+ㅠ=듀 (dyu)   ㄹ+ㅠ=류 (ryu)

ㄱ+ㅡ=그 (geu)   ㄴ+ㅡ=느 (neu)   ㄷ+ㅡ=드 (deu)   ㄹ+ㅡ=르 (reu)

ㄱ+ㅣ=기 (gi)   ㄴ+ㅣ=니 (ni)   ㄷ+ㅣ=디 (di)   ㄹ+ㅣ=리 (ri)

As the above examples clearly show, *Hangeul*, with only 14 consonants and 10 vowels, is capable of expressing virtually any sound.

The Korean language has a well-developed and expansive vocabulary, and therefore, it is very difficult to express fully in foreign letter.

However, due to its scientific design, it is quite easy to approximate the sounds of foreign words in the Korean alphabet. Following are some examples of English words expressed in *Hangeul*.

London	New York	Hong Kong
런 던	뉴 욕	홍 콩

I	am	a	boy
아이	앰	어	보이

Good	morning
굿	모닝

With a large number of programs written in *Hangeul*, people can incorporate computers into their lives without difficulty.

In particular, because of its simplicity and the rather small number of letters, *Hangeul* is very easy for children or speakers of other languages to learn.

Most children are capable of expressing their feelings and thoughts by the ages of two or three, albeit in primitive form. However, most Korean children by the time they reach school age, have mastered *Hangeul*, which is unusual. This fact clearly attests to the easy learnability and accessibility of the Korean alphabet.

It is ironic that the strongest proof of the easy learnability of the alphabet came from the critics who argued against the creation of *Hunminjeongeum*. Some scholars vehemently voiced their views against the "new" alphabet because of its learnability, and in derision, they called it *Achimgeul* (morning letters) or *Amgeul* (women's letters).

Achimgeul meant that it could be learned in one morning. For those scholars who had spent years in learning the complicated ideographs of the Chinese language, *Hangeul* did not appear to be worthy of learning. *Amgeul* meant that even women who had no academic training or background around the time *Hangeul* was invented could easily learn the alphabet. Back then there were those who considered the pursuit of academic studies and the subject of reading and writing to be the sole domain of a few privileged scholars.

Such misconceptions were the result of confusing simple linguistic learning with more advanced academic studies. Without learning the basic alphabet, reading and writing would be impossible, let alone the study of more advanced subjects. Without being able to read and write, there can be no indirect communication of one's feelings and thoughts. Surely, King Sejong's intent was to enrich the lives of the people by introducing *Hangeul*, and not to make scholars out of all his subjects.

In subsequent history, *Hangeul* has been a mainstay of Korean culture, helping preserve the country's national identity and independence.

Illiteracy is virtually nonexistent in Korea. This is another fact that attests to the easy learnability of *Hangeul*. It is not uncommon for a foreigner to gain a working knowledge of *Hangeul* after one or two hours of intensive studying. In addition, because of its scientific design, *Hangeul* lends itself to easy mechanization. In this age of computers, many people now are able to incorporate computers into their lives without difficulties, thanks to a large number of programs written in *Hangeul*.

Because *Hangeul* is simple and easy to learn, illiteracy is virtually nonexistent in Korea. *Hangeul* calligraphy is an art.

Jeryeak

The Music of the Jongmyo Ancestral Rites

Koreans, in keeping with Confucian tenets, continue to revere their ancestors and to honor their achievements. This is most clearly evident on first Sunday in every May when the descendants of the Jeonju Yi Royal Family honor Korea's past royalty in elaborate Confucian rites at Jongmyo, the royal ancestral shrine of the Joseon Dynasty.

Dressed in black robes and colorful aprons embroidered with animals signifying their rank and wearing hats run through with long horizontal pins, elderly men offer libations of food and drink before the spirit tablets of the kings that ruled Korea from 1392 to 1910. While they do so, young, scarlet-clad women perfectly aligned in a square of eight rows by eight rows slowly bend and sway. Each one gently lifts a foot shod in black felt and, turning first to the east and then to the west and the north, bends slightly. They alternately put on a round red cap and a black one

A traditional Korean orchestra playing at Jongmyo (the Royal Ancestral Shrine) of the Joseon Dynasty (1392-1910)

according to the sequence of the dances. They strike a symbolic ax against a wooden shield for the military dances and wave a flute adorned with a dragon head and pheasant feathers for the civil dances. The *ilmu*, as this kind of dance is called, is characterized by a repetition of simple and restrained movements expressing humility and reverence. It is performed to the accompaniment of orchestras of musicians clothed in magenta robes who draw exotic sounds from ancient instruments of stone, metal, wood, leather and silk.

It is a colorful pageant but probably not nearly as grand as in the days of old when the rites, called *jehyang* or *jerye*, were performed several times a year and lasted all day. At that time, the day began in the early dawn with the king selecting the food offerings from choice cows,

Sixty-four dancers performing part of the ritual at Jongmyo.

The *Munmu* (Civil Dance) honors the literary and scholarly achievements of the royal ancestors.

goats and pigs as well as the finest fruits, grains and honey brought to the capital from every province.

Although today's ceremony, which starts around ten o'clock in the morning, is of a much-abbreviated form, it is a rare opportunity to experience the pomp and ceremony that characterized the highly Confucian Dynasty of Joseon. In the past, the king, the civil and military court officials, and other lesser nobles performed the rites with the court's musicians and dancers providing the accompaniment. Today the members of the Jeonju Yi Royal Family Association perform the rites to the accompaniment of music and dance provided by musicians from the National Center for Korean Traditional Performing Arts and dancers from the Korean Traditional Music National High School.

As many as 19 different classical Korean and Chinese musical instruments including stone chimes, bronze bells, various drums and other percussion instruments, and wind and string instruments are used during the ceremony. They are arranged in two orchestras that perform antiphonally: the terrace orchestra or *deungga* situated on the terrace of the shrine; and, the ground orchestra or *heonga*, situated in the courtyard. During the time of Joseon, the *deungga* was made up of one singer and 36 musicians and the *heonga*, 72 musicians but nowadays the two orchestras number some 50 in all.

The music, called *jeryeak*, dates to the reign of King Sejong (r. 1418-1450), who ordered the court's music master to restore the ritual music to its original Chinese Zhou Dynasty form because it

The music performance at Jongmyo is performed by the *heonga* (the orchestra in the courtyard) and the *deungga* (the orchestra on the terrace).

had changed considerably since its introduction from China around 1116 when King Yejong of the Goryeo Dynasty (918-1392) began using Chinese musical instruments and music at the royal ancestral rites. It is not known what type of music was used before then but historical records indicate that memorial rites for royal ancestors were performed as early as A.D. 6 in the court of the Silla Kingdom (57 B.C.-A.D. 935). King Sejong wanted to replace the Chinese music with native Korean music in the belief that the spirits of the deceased kings would prefer the music they had enjoyed while alive. He revised musical arrangements and ordered new compositions made but he faced opposition from his courtiers who insisted on using Chinese music. In 1464,

A court musician playing the *pyeonjong*, a set of 16 bells.

An official pouring wine to offer to the spirit of the king. (right)

Officials line up for the memorial rite at Jongmyo. (left)

King Sejo had *Botaepyeong* and *Jeongdaeeop*, two pieces composed by King Sejong, included in the score for the royal ancestral rites and they have been a part of the rites ever since. The *deungga* plays *Botaepyeong*, which praises the civil achievements of the kings, and the *heonga* plays *Jeongdaeeop*, which praises the kings' military exploits and achievements. The songs invite the ancestral spirits to descend from heaven to enjoy the offerings and to grant blessings on their posterity. The songs also recount the kings' achievements in founding the Dynasty and defending the country in order to encourage their descendants to follow in their footsteps.

As the stately, though somewhat ponderous, music is played, the officiants offer wine in brass cups to each spirit three times. An invocation is read for each spirit with the offering of the first cup of wine. The wine and food offerings are on tables before the spirit tablets in the cubicles of the

Officials entering Jongmyo carry the memorial tablets of the kings of the Joseon Dynasty (previous page)

shrine. There are two wine cups for each occupant of the cubicles; for example, on the table before King Sungjong's cubicle are six wine cups, two for the king, and two for each of his wives, Queen Min and Queen Yun. During the time of Joseon, the king offered the first cup of wine, the crown prince the second and the chief state minister the third. Upon completion of the rites, the king drank wine removed from the altar of Taejo, the Dynasty's founder, as a gesture of communion with his spirit.

There are 19 cubicles in Jeongjeon and 16 in Yeongnyeongjeon, Jongmyo 's two main buildings. Jeongjeon, the main hall, houses the spirit tablets of the kings of outstanding achievements and those who left direct heirs to the throne. Yeongnyeongjeon, Hall of Eternal Peace, houses the tablets of lesser monarchs and those who died without direct heirs or who were honored posthumously with the title of king. The spirit of each king is allotted a cubicle. On the far side of the cubicle is a high chair-like table on which the wooden spirit tablet bearing the king's name is enshrined. In front of the table is a space just large enough for a person to make a prostrate, head-to-floor bow. The cubicles also contain a list of each king's achievements and his personal seal and favorite books as well as the spirit tablets of all his queens.

Taejo, the founder-king of the Joseon Dynasty; Sejong, who is credited with the invention of the Korean alphabet; and Gojong and Sunjong, the last rulers of Joseon, are among the kings

Jongmyo (the Royal Ancestral Shrine) was put on the UNESCO World Cultural Heritage List in 1995. The shrine comes to life once a year when descendants of the royal family of the Joseon Dynasty (1392-1910) gather to observe memorial rites for theirancestors. (previous page).

Officials preparing for a rite at Jongmyo

enshrined in Jeongjeon. The child-king Danjong and the last crown prince, Yeongwang, who died in 1970, are among those honored in Yeong-nyeongjeon. The tablets of the father, grandfather, great-grandfather and great-great-grandfather of Taejo are also enshrined in Yeongnyeongjeon, along with those of their wives.

An unusually long building with wings at either side and a straight, uninterrupted roof, Jeongjeon stands on a terrace and is fronted by a large raised cobbled plaza. It was first built in 1395 by King Taejo when he moved his capital from Gaeseong, a city in North Korea, to

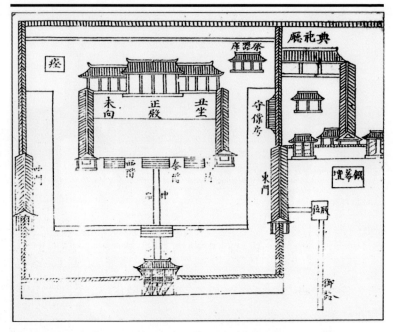

A blueprint for Jongmyo.

Hanyang, today's Seoul. In keeping with the traditional Chinese model, it was situated to the southeast of the main palace, *Gyeongbokgung*, and the altar for the gods of earth and harvest, *Sajikdan*, to the southwest of the palace so that the ancestral shrine would be on the king's left when seated on the throne and *Sajikdan* altar on his right. It was enlarged during the reign of King Myeongjong (r. 1545-1567), destroyed during the 1592-1598 Japanese invasions, and rebuilt by King Gwanghaegun in 1608. It was enlarged by King Yeongjo (r. 1724-1776), again by King Heonjong (r. 1834-1849), and finally to its present size by King Gojong (r. 1863-1907). Forty-nine tablets are enshrined here.

Yeongnyeongjeon (Hall of Eternal Peace) at Jongmyo.

A court orchestra
playing traditional
music during the rite.

Rows of officials performing the rite.

Yeongnyeongjeon is similar to Jeongjeon, but the center, which houses the tablets of Taejo's ancestors, is raised higher than the wings. It was constructed in 1421 by King Sejong. Burnt down during the Japanese invasions, it was reconstructed by King Gwanghaegun in 1608 and later enlarged. Thirty-four tablets are enshrined in it now.

Both buildings are of a simple, austere architectural style marked by thick wood columns and sharply pitched roofs that are covered with traditional gray tiles. Ceramic animal figures, symbolic guardians of the buildings, adorn the ridges of the roofs.

Near the front of the courtyard of Jeongjeon is a structure called *Gongsindang*. It houses the tablets of 83 ministers of state and others recognized for meritorious service. Other structures inside Jongmyo include a place for the king and crown prince to bathe and dress in preparation for the rites, a building for the musicians to rest and rehearse, and a kitchen to prepare the foods and utensils necessary for the memorial rites. The walkways leading to the various structures are raised in the center. The king would use the center and the lesser nobles the sides but now the chief officiant of the rites uses the center.

Throughout the Joseon period, memorial rites were held five times a year for the spirits of the kings enshrined in Jeongjeon and twice a year for those enshrined in Yeongnyeongjeon. The rites were abolished in the early part of the 20th century when Korea was under Japanese colonial

rule but were resumed in 1969, though in the form of one large service. Jeonju Yi Royal Family Association has held the service at Jongmyo on first Sunday in every May since 1971.

Building shrines to honor deceased rulers was a time-honored tradition in ancient China, Korea, Japan, Vietnam and other East Asian countries that were within the Chinese cultural sphere where Confucianism developed into the fundamental ruling ideology. Royal ancestral rites were of great national importance, especially in China and Korea where centralized monarchies prevailed for centuries.

Jongmyo is the oldest and most authentic of the royal shrines that have been preserved. Consecrated to the Joseon Dynasty and its forebears, it has existed in its current form since the 16th century and ritual ceremonies linking rites, music and dance are still held there, perpetuating a tradition that goes back to the 14th century. Jongmyo 's importance is enhanced by the persistence there of important elements of Intangible Cultural Heritage in the form of traditional ritual practices and forms including the *jeryeak* royal ancestral shrine music. For all these reasons, Jongmyo was added to the UNESCO World Cultural Heritage List, recognizing it as a cultural asset for all humanity.

Officials carrying the royal tablets entering Jongmyo.

Masks and Mask Dance-Dramas

M asks are called *tal* in Korean, but they are also known by many other names such as *gamyeon, gwangdae, chorani, talbak* and *talbagaji*. Korean masks come with black cloth attached to the sides of the mask designed to cover the back of the head and also to simulate black hair. *Talchum*, which literally means "mask dance," is not just a dance performed by masked dancers but also a drama with masked characters enacting persons, animals or supernatural beings.

Masks and mask dances developed in Korea as early as the Prehistoric age. The masks can be categorized in two kinds: religious masks and artistic masks. Some masks were enshrined in shaman shrines and revered with periodical offering rites. Other religious masks were used to expel evil spirits, like *Bangsangsi,* which until recently, were seen at the forefront of a funeral procession to ward off evil spirits. Artistic masks were mostly used in dance and drama. However,

Masks and mask dances date back to prehistoric times in Korea. Shown here are various masks used in the *Gangnyeong* mask dance.

these also had religious functions to some extent.

Most Korean *tal* are solid but some have movable parts like the eyeballs of the *Bang-sangsi* mask, the mouth of the lion mask and the winking eyes of some masks in dance-drama. Of special note are the masks featured in a mask dance-drama developed in the Hahoe region. They are made out of two pieces, with the chin coming in a separate piece and attached to the upper part with strings. They have a great advantage of their expression.

Tal are not only characterized by their respective roles but also reflect the expressions and bone structures of Korean faces. Their shapes are grotesque and greatly exaggerated, and their colors are deep and bright. This is because *talchum*, the mask dance-drama, was usually performed at night in the light from wood fires. Masks less powerful in expression and color would have failed to deliver the themes of the drama. Religious masks and masks for daytime performances were much less vivid.

Masks are made of paper, wood, gourd and

A mask for the monk in Hahoe *byeolsingut* mask dance (above).
Hahoe *byeolsingut* mask dance-drama (left).

81

fur. Paper masks and gourd masks are prevalent, because they are simpler to make and also because they are lightweight and thus convenient to dance with.

Red, black, white and other primal colors are favored for effective characterization of the masks. The colors also identify the gender and age of the characters. An old person's mask is black, whereas that of a young man is red and that of a young woman white. In the traditional philosophy of identifying colors with directions and seasons, the black stands for the north and winter whereas the red stands for the south and summer. In many of the *talchum* dramas, the young man always wins over the old in a

4

5

Korean masks are quite striking in appearance and vivid in color.

1. *Chwibari*, an old bachelor (*Bongsan talchum*).
2. *Somu*, a young shaman (*Yangju byeolsandae* mask dance-drama).
3. *Yeonnip*, a high monk (*Songpa sandae* drama).
4. *Hongbaek yangban*, red/white aristocrat (*Goseong ogwangdae* mask dance).
5. *Gaksi*, a young woman (*Hahoe pyeolsingut* mask dance).

symbolic gesture of the summer triumphing over the winter. In this sense, *talchum* is a vestige of fertility rites.

Most of the masks depict human faces but some represent deities, and there are also masks of animals, real and imagined. An interesting feature is that the masks of *yangban*, the upper class gentlemen, are almost always deformed in one way or another with harelips, sometimes cleaved in both upper and lower lips, a lopsided mouth, a distorted nose or squint eyes–a reflection of the commoners' hostility toward the privileged class.

Mask dance-dramas are basically a folk art naturally developed among the common people of Joseon society(1392-1910). They vary slighty according to region and performer but they all share fundamental characteristics. They are

based on a sense of rebellion felt by the common people toward the reality of their lives. Their basic themes are exorcism rites, ritual dances or biting satire and parody of human weaknesses, social evils and privileged class. Like the folk literature of the time, it appeals to its audiences by ridiculing apostate Buddhist monks, decadent noblemen, and shamans. The conflict between an ugly wife and a seductive concubine is another popular theme.

The mask dance-drama consists of several acts, but they are quite different from the acts in modern plays. They are a loose presentation of

Yangju byeolsandae mask dance-drama. Masks are used to represent a variety of characters in the mask dance and to create a dramatic effect (previous page).

Mask dances were performed in a *madang* or outdoor arena.
Dongnae deulloleum mask dance.

several different episodes in an omnibus style. Because the lines of the actors have been passed on in oral tradition, they are quite flexible and subject to improvisation. The dance part also can be lengthened or shortened freely, so that the entire performance can take anywhere between three or four hours to the whole night until daybreak.

With regional variations, the mask dance-drama was generally performed on the First Full Moon, Buddha's Birthday on the Eighth of the Fourth Moon, Dano Festival and *Chuseok*. It was also performed at festive occasions of the state or

Koreans enjoy mask dances, that use a wide variety of masks. Masks are still made today.

at rituals to supplicate for rain.

Traditionally, Korean mask dance-drama was always performed outdoors. During Goryeo and Joseon periods, it was performed on an improvised stage called *sandae* or up on a sloped incline so that the audience in their seats below could see well. There was a screened area used as a dressing room to the left of the stage and musicians sat to right of the stage. Actors were all males until *gisaeng*, female entertainers, joined them in modern times to take up the role of

Mask dance, or *talchum*, is a form of folk drama enjoyed by the common people.
A scene from the *Bongsan talchum* (left).

shamans and concubines.

Lively dance accompanied by vigorous music from three string and six wind and percussion instruments take up the major part of a mask dance-drama performance, with actors stopping to deliver their lines with a great deal of gesticulation. Many of the roles do not have any dialogue of their own but act in pantomime, their extraordinarily stylized masks delivering the dramatic impact of their characters. The dance enlivens the drama and functions to round up each scene but is also performed without any regard to the progress of the plot.

The most remarkable feature of Korean mask dance-drama is the enthusiastic participation of the audience. Toward the end of a performance there is little distinction between the actors and the audience as they join together in robust dance and bring it to a truly affirmative life-enhancing finale. In Korean mask dance-drama, the common people could vent their frustrations through comic dramatization and enliven their lives with a collective experience of ecstasy.

A mask dance, which is rich in history,
is performed in Daehangno, an area of Seoul
known as a gathering place for young people.

Taekwondo

T aekwondo is an officially acknowledged international sport originated in Korea and is today practiced worldwide. Taekwondo uses the whole body, particularly the hands and feet. It not only strengthens one's physique, but also cultivates character via physical and mental training. Coupled with techniques of discipline, taekwondo is a self-defense martial art.

The evidence of taekwondo's existence as a systemized defense operation using the body's instinctive reflexes can be traced back to ceremonial games that were performed during religious events in the era of the ancient tribal states. During religious ceremonies such as *Yeonggo* and *Dongmaeng* (a sort of thanksgiving ceremony), and *Mucheon* (Dance to Heaven), ancient Koreans performed a unique exercise for physical training. This exercise was the original inception of taekwondo.

With this historical background, taekwondo (also known by its older name, *taekkyeon*) secured the status of Korean's traditional martial art.

Taekwondo is the only officially acknowledged international sport originated in Korea. Exhibition by high-grade holders.

During the Three Kingdoms period, *taekkyeon* became a required military art; the martial art was emphasized to enhance national defense and battle capabilities, and was practiced in the *Musadan* (a military organization) that was responsible for national defense.

Examples of *Musadan* are the *Seonbae* of Goguryeo and the *Hwarang* of Silla. *Seonbae*, which was founded during the era of King Taejo of Goguryeo, practiced *taekkyeon* (also called *taekgoni*) to strengthen their country's defense capabilities. Strengthening this claim is a mural in the *Muyongchong* (Tomb of the Dancers) in southern Manchuria. Drawn on the ceiling of the burial chamber and the master chamber of the tomb was a vivid scene of a *taekkyeon* match.

Taekkyeon was practiced in Silla in order to

A *taekkyeon* (an older name for taekwondo) match painted on a mural from the Goguryeo era (37 B.C.-A.D. 668).

reinforce national development, and was the basic martial art of the *Hwarang* (Flower of Youth Corps). Evidence attesting to *taekkyeon's* role during the Silla period can be found in the *Geumgangyeoksasang* (a guardian of a temple gate), which is now housed in the Gyeongju National Museum.

The aforementioned traditions were continuously superseded and further developed during the Goryeo period. The value of *taekkyeon* as a martial art for the defense and prosperity of the nation was acknowledged, and as a consequence, its standards were raised, leading to further systemization and popularity. Among King Uijong's writings is a record stating that Yi Uimin was promoted because of his outstanding *taekkyeon* techniques. The record also shows that Choe Chungheon threw banquets and let strong men from the *Jungbang* (Council of

One of the basic movements of *taekkyeon* as shown by a *Geumgangyeoksasang* (one of a pair of door guardians of a Buddhist temple) from the Silla period (57 B.C.-A.D. 935).

Generals) compete against each other in *taekkyeon* matches; winners from the match were awarded with government posts. Finally, there is a record about Byeon Anyeol's winning matches against Im Gyeonmi and Yeom Heungbang and being promoted from assistant-head to head of the Royal Secretariat as a reward. Such evidence implies that the value of taekwondo as a martial art was acknowledged in the Goryeo Dynasty at the national level, while also confirming the existence of clear judging criteria for competitions.

The basic movements of taekwondo are included in *Muyedobotongji* (Comprehensive Illustrated Manual of Martial Arts), written during the Joseon era(1392-1910).

Based on this information, it can be deduced that taekwondo, as a military art, had reached a level of high performance during the Goryeo

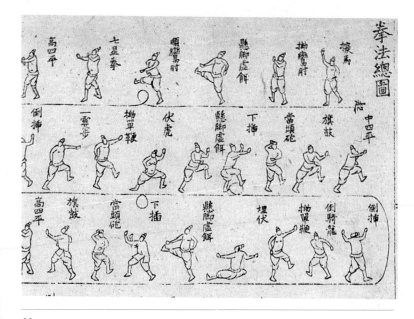

Taekkyeon and wrestling are depicted in this picture entitled *Taekwaedo* (Portrait of Valor) by Yu Suk, a late Joseon era painter.

period. A number of written entries, such as "the rafter was moved when Yi Uimin hit the pillar with his bare fist," or "the wall was broken when Du Gyeongseung hit the wall with his fist" substantiate the high and sometimes lethal level of taekwondo standards at that time. Another record states, "Yi Uimin punched a man's backbone and killed him."

With the advent of explosives and the appearance of new weapons by the end of the Goryeo era, however, taekwondo, which was highly supported at the national level during the beginning and middle periods of the Goryeo Dynasty, received a steadily declining level of support. As a result of its weakened function as a martial art, the sport was transformed into a folk game at one point. According to records in the *Goryeosa* (History of Goryeo, 1454), people who gambled on *taekkyeon* for money or material goods were punished by 100 strokes of a paddle; a house owner who provided boarding or gambling money to gamblers also received the same number of paddle beatings as punishment. Such records imply that *taekkyeon* was enjoyed as a folk game by many people and was deeply rooted in Koreans' lives.

Later, during the Joseon era, military arts regained their prominence due to political circumstances in the early period of the Dynasty's foundation and the need for national defense. People who were skilled in *taekkyeon* received preferable treatment, and *taekkyeon* was chosen as a military art. Documents show that during the selection of military soldiers by the Uiheungbu (a military command) during the 10th year (1410) of King Taejong, persons who had beaten three rivals in *taekkyeon* matches were selected to become *bangpyeguns* (shielding soldiers). In the following year, skills in *taekkyeon* were applied as a major criterion for recruiting soldiers. This practice attracted to the military service many of the *gwanno*, male provincial government slaves, who by virtue of their work were mostly well versed in the martial art.

Once the country's organizational structure

Gyeokpa
(breaking boards)

Main techniques of taekwondo:

Araemakgi

Sonnalchigi

Yeopjireugi

Yeopchagi

Bandalchagi

was solidified, nonetheless, the importance of the martial art was again deemphasized due to the unavoidable strengthening of the power of the literati. However, this trend was reversed when the country experienced severe difficulties such as the *Imjinwaeran* (the Japanese invasion of Joseon) in 1592 and the *Byeongjahoran* (the Manchu invasion) in 1636. At the national level, the *Hullyeondogam* (Military Training Command) was established to support martial arts. *Muye dobotongji*, a text for martial art, was written by Yi Deokmu and Bak Jega. Such national support enabled *taekkyeon* to regain its vitality as a martial art and folk game.

In *Donggungnyeojiseungnam* (Augmented Survey of the Geography of Korea), it is stated that in one of the towns in Eunjin-hyeon in Chungcheong-do province, people from the Chungcheong-do and Jeolla-do provinces gathered around on Buddhist All Souls' Day to compete in *taekkyeon* matches, while in the *pungsokhwa* (genre pictures) of that period scenes of *taekkyeon* can often be found. Based on this evidence, it is clear that *taekkyeon* was quite popular and deeply rooted in the daily lives of Koreans.

Taekwondo is now firmly established as an international sport.

With time's passage, methods of national defense changed, along with peoples' altitudes. Consequently, *taekkyeon* became primarily a folk match or game rather than a military art. With Japan's undisguised intention of invading Korea, however, *taekkyeon* emerged as a national pastime. The fact that it was already established

as a folk game, coupled with the Koreans' consciousness of being a homogeneous nation distinct from the Japanese, fueled their passion for the art.

During the period when Japan controlled Korea, *taekkyeon* was suppressed. Nevertheless, it was secretly passed on among certain *taekkyeon* masters even during this period.

After national independence in 1945, *taekkyeon's* revitalization began once again, aided by restored personal freedoms. It was during this period that a new word, "taekwon," was coined and began to be widely used. Concurrently, the characteristics of the master-trainee relationship in taekwondo changed to emphasize the characteristics of taekwondo as more of a sport than a martial art. With the foundation of the Korea Taekwondo Association in September of 1961, taekwondo officially became a sport .

In 1962, the Korea Taekwondo Association became a member organization of the Korea Amateur Sports Association, and the following year taekwondo was chosen as a regular entry for the National Sports Festival. In 1971 taekwondo's outstanding value was acknowledged, and taekwondo was recognized as a national sport; today there are about 3,700 taekwondo practice halls and approximately 10,000 masters in Korea, along with 3,000,000 grade-holders and 3,500,000 trainees.

In 1971, the Korea Taekwondo Association established etiquette criteria to guide those practicing taekwondo. The criteria include the areas of etiquette and attitude, articles to follow in daily living places and in practice halls, dress code and personal appearance guidelines to be followed when conversing or visiting someone. The Gukgiwon was opened in 1972 to function as the central practice hall and competition stadium for taekwondo.

The first World Taekwondo Championship was held in Seoul during 1973, at which time the World Taekwondo Federation was founded. The World Taekwondo Federation eventually became a member of the GAISF(General Association of International Sports Federations), and was chosen as an official entry by the Committee for the International Soldiers Meet (CISM) in 1976. Today, the World Taekwondo Federation has 153 member countries, and 3,000 masters have been dispatched to these countries to instruct approximately 50 million trainees worldwide.

The sport's steady progress and growth were responsible for taekwondo's selection as a demonstration sport for the Olympic Games at the General Assembly of the International Olympic Committee on July 15, 1980. During the General Assembly of the International Olympic Committee in 1981, taekwondo was also chosen for inclusion in the 10th Asian Games. Having been selected as a demonstration sport for the 1988 Olympic Games, taekwondo firmly established its presence in the international sports arena.

The First International Taekwondo Academic Conference, which was held in Seoul in

December 1983, was another event which greatly contributed to the development of taekwondo. Partially as a result of the heightened worldwide interest in taekwondo demonstrated by this event, it was decided during the International Olympic Committee meeting held in Sydney, Australia, that taekwondo was an official entry in the 2000 Sydney Olympic Games.

The training methods of taekwondo can be differentiated into *gibondongjak, pumse, gyeorugi, dallyeon,* and *hosinsul.* The *gibondongjak* (basic movements) refer to dynamic elements of the use of hands and feet and are the basis of taekwondo. They include *chigi* (striking) techniques by use of fists and the outer side of the hand. *Pumse* refers to training that is done alone with an imaginary counterpart. Following the drill line, one practices to master effective techniques of attack and defense movements so as to improve one's readiness, muscular power, flexibility, ability to shift one's center of power, control of breathing, and speed of movement. Types of *pumse* include *Taegeuk* (1-8 *jang*) and *Palgwae* (1-8 *jang*) for non-grade-holders, and *Goryeo, Geumgang, Taebaek, Pyeongwon, Sipjin, Jitae, Cheonggwon, Hansu,* and *Ilyeo* for grade-holders.

Gyeorugi, an application of *Pumse* to an actual situation in order to demonstrate techniques of attack and defense, is divided into two parts: *machueogyeorugi* and *gyeorugi. Machueogyeorugi*

Nopichagi (high kick)

refs to a synchronized demonstration of given attack and defense techniques, while *gyeorugi* refers to the free application of those techniques to an opponent's vulnerable areas. The latter enhances one's spirit of fighting and courage.

Dallyeon involves strengthening body parts such as one's hands and feet, through the use of various equipment, in order to increase one's power for attack and defense, while *hosinsul* consists of techniques to defeat a rival's attack and effectively counterattack.

Taekwondo matches are held according to weight categories. These categories include finweight, flyweight, bantamweight, featherweight, welter-weight, middleweight, and heavyweight. The time allotted for a match is three three-minute rounds, with a one minute rest between rounds.

The competition floor is a square with sides of a total length of eight meters. A mattress is placed on the floor. For the safety of the competitor, protective pads for certain parts of the body, such as the torso and head, are worn over the competition outfit. Judging is carried out by one examiner, one chief referee, and four sub-referees.

The power and grace of taekwondo was demonstrated during the opening ceremony of the 1988 Seoul Olympic Games.

Korean Ginseng

G inseng is a medicinal plant with wondrous powers. Although it grows in other countries as well, it is widely cultivated in Korea where the climate and soil produce the world's finest. It is a perennial herb that belongs to the *Araliaceae* family. Scientifically it is known as *Panax schinseng Nees*.

A ginseng plant usually grows to be about 60cm tall. The subterranean stem is short, and stands either straight or slightly tilted. The root looks similar to that of a Chinese bellflower, with a single stalk growing out the stem. Three or four leaves grow at the end of the stalk. Light-green flowers blossom in April. When the flowers wither away, they are replaced by round, reddish fruit.

To distinguish it from ginseng grown in other parts of the world, Korean-grown ginseng is specifically called "Goryeo ginseng," named after the ancient dynasty of Goryeo from which the nation's current English name "Korea" is derived. Even in the old days, Korean ginseng used a different Chinese character for *"sam"*

Korean ginseng is the world's finest in quality and effectiveness.

(meaning ginseng): "蔘"was used for other types, while "參" was reserved for Korean ginseng.

Ginseng grown in the wild, deep in the mountains, is known as *sansam* (mountain ginseng). It is, however, found only rarely, and cultivation meets nearly all of the demand these days. Goryeo ginseng's reputation began with sansam. In the old day, the search for it was almost a spiritual endeavor for those dwelling in the nation's mountainous regions. Even today, there are those who spend their lives wandering around deep valleys for the mystical plant. They are known as *simmani* or *simmemani* (both mean "gatherer of wild ginseng").

The territory of the kingdom of Goguryeo (37 B.C.-A.D.668) extended north to the Liaodong

A *simmani* is showing a *sansam* found deep in the mountains (above). *Sansam*, known as a mysterious cure, is also frequently depicted in paintings portraying immortals (right).

region of China, Manchuria, and the coastal provinces of Siberia. Wild ginseng grew in these regions as well as on the Korean Peninsula. Goguryeo had a virtual monopoly on the supply of ginseng in those days. Since then, the preeminence of Goryeo ginseng has continued to this day. In modern times, Koreans have developed unique cultivation, treatment, and merchandising techniques to preserve the nation's honor as the home of the world's finest ginseng. The constitution of ginseng changes with climate and soil conditions. Thus, the quality of Goryeo ginseng is different from those of other types, so much so that it has its own scientific name.

Ginseng grown in America is called American, western, *Gwangdong, Hwagi,* or Po ginseng ; *Panax quinquefolium* Linne is the scientific term. Japan's ginseng is *Panax japonicum* C.A. Meyer, and China's *Panax notoginseng* (Burk) F.H. Chen. They all belong to the *araliaceae* family, but are fundamentally different from Goryeo ginseng. Siberian ginseng, which is widely sold in Europe and America these days, also belongs to the same family, but not to the *Panax* (ginseng) genus. It is the root of a shrub, known by its scientific name, *Eleutherococcus senticosus* Maxim. Ginseng is very sensitive to climate and soil, and is thus extremely difficult to cultivate. Different locations of cultivation make for vastly different shapes, qualities, and medicinal powers. Hence, ginseng grown in other countries can hardly match Korean ginseng.

Ginseng fruit (abov and ginseng farm (righ

Ginseng cultivation in Korea began centuries ago, according to historical materials found in Korea and elsewhere. *Pents'ao kangmu* (Korean: *Bonchogangmok;* Encyclopedia of Herbs), 52 volumes on the medicinal properties of plants, minerals and insects, was begun in 1552 and published in 1590 by a Ming Chinese scholar named Li Shizhen. It details how people at that time grew and traded ginseng. Some ancient Korean compilations of folk wisdom and mythology indicate that even as early as the fifth century, ginseng had begun to be cultivated from strains collected in the wild. Another record refers to the existence of ginseng cultivation in the eighth century during the Silla Kingdom (57B.C.-A.D.935). Still another states that ginseng cultivation was widely practiced in the days of King Gojong (1213-1259) during the Goryeo Dynasty.

Taken together, these materials indicate that ginseng cultivation originated in the area around Mt. Mohusan in the township of *Dongbok* in an area which is now a part of Jeollanam-do province. It was quickly picked up by the enterprising merchants of Gaeseong, the capital of Goryeo who introduced *Dongbok* ginseng to the residents of the capital, and the area around Gaeseong quickly became the center of ginseng cultivation.

Korea's expertise in cultivation, coupled with perfect weather and soil conditions, has made Korean ginseng a prized product on the global market. The following are the optimum

Ginseng, grown with hard work and devotion, is traded in the market.

conditions for ginseng cultivation.

1. Temperature: 9-13.8⁰C yearly average; 20-25⁰C during the summer. Physiological defects appear at around 35⁰C.

2. Precipitation: 700-2,000 mm yearly (1,100-1,300 mm optimum). Relatively small snowfall desirable.

3. Lighting: diffused lighting at 1/8 to 1/13 of the strength of natural outside light. Direct sunlight is detrimental to ginseng.

4. Soil: sandy top soil and clay deep soil with plenty of potassium.

5. Location: 5-15° slope in north/northeastern direction. (Or level land that drains well)

6. Other conditions that simulate the environment for ginseng grown in the wild, such as a thick accumulation of decaying foliage. Extensive use of chemical fertilizers

Ginseng is cleaned at a ginseng processing factory (above).

International ginseng symposiums are frequently held in Korea, the leading exporter of ginseng.

makes the soil unnatural and thus unfit for ginseng.

By nature, the climate and soil of Korean Peninsula meet all of the above conditions. Thus, ginseng can be grown in almost all regions of the country.

The medicinal powers of ginseng are extensively discussed in numerous historic materials. In *Shennung pents'ao ching* (Korean: *Sinnong Bonchogyeong*; Shen Nung's Pharmacopoeia), China's oldest written book on herbs, it is noted that ginseng protects the digestive system, calms the nerves, clears the eyes, and, if taken over a long period of time, makes the body light and agile.

Ginseng is used as a restorative or tonic, rather than as a cure for a particular illness. Traditional East Asian medicine officially lists the following effects of ginseng: strengthening of organs; stimulation of the heart; protection of the stomach and enhancement of stamina; and calming of nerves. As such, it is routinely prescribed to people with weak digestive systems and poorly functioning metabolisms. People with stomach discomfort, chronic indigestion, heartburn, emesis, and poor appetite can greatly benefit from ginseng.

Scientific research on the effects of ginseng took off in the 1950s in both pharmaceutical and clinical studies, unveiling the mystery that had surrounded the plant for thousands of years. Korean scholars have made great contributions to the scientific inquiries into ginseng. They have consolidated the nation's reputation as the home of ginseng in every aspect– cultivation, treatment and merchandising, and even research.

Acccording to existing studies, the primary ingredient that gives ginseng its medicinal quality is saponin, which reduces fatigue, enhances the body's productivity, stimulates the development of sexual glands and brings down the blood sugar level. In recent theoretical analyses, ginseng's basic medical action is presumed to be that of an adaptogen, enhancing the overall resistance of the body and facilitating its normalization

and recovery from a state of illness. More specifically, ginseng facilitates the production of glucocorticoid, an adrenocortical hormone, strengthening the ability of the adrenal cortex to deal with various kinds of stress to the body.

By stimulating the cerebral cortex and the choline, ginseng also brings down blood pressure, facilitates breathing, reduces excess sugar in the blood, assists the actions of insulin, increases red blood cells and hemoglobin, and strengthens the digestive tract. Active research is underway to prove that ginseng also facilitates the formation of bio protein and DNA, and suppresses cancer.

Indeed, science is confirming the age-old belief that ginseng is the elixir of life. Thus, ginseng is a central ingredient in numerous prescriptions in traditional East Asian medicine. In Korea, where its wondrous powers were accepted long before modern science came into existence, it is also drunk as a tea or a liquor.

World-class ginseng tea, ginseng capsules, and other ginseng products.

Bulguksa Temple and Seokguram

L ocated about 16 kilometers southeast of downtown Gyeongju, a town that was once the capital of the ancient Silla Kingdom(57 B.C.-A.D. 935), is Bulguksa, one of the largest and most beautiful Buddhist temples in Korea. Built on a series of stone terraces, Bulguksa temple appears to emerge organically from the rocky terrain of the wooded foothills of Mt. Tohamsan. This is because it was built in accordance with ancient notions of architecture and principles of geomancy that man-made structures should not be obtrusive but should harmonize with the surroundings. It is both monolithic and intricate and takes on different guises as the light and shadows shift and the weather changes.

Bulguksa temple dates to a small temple that King Beopheung (r. 514-540), Silla's 23rd monarch and the first Silla ruler to embrace Buddhism, had erected for his queen to pray for

The entrance to Bulguksa temple seen from the side.

the prosperity and peace of the kingdom. Its present structures, however, date to 751 when Kim Daeseong, a devoted Buddhist who had served as chief state minister, began building the large "Temple of the Buddha Land." An able administrator with an eye for beauty, Kim directed the construction until his death in 774, a few years before the project was completed. Originally consisting of more than 80 buildings, 10 times the number surviving today, it was the center of Silla Buddhism and served primarily as a place to pray for the Buddha's protection against invaders. The temple's stonework

A bird's-eye view of the Bulguksa temple compound (left).

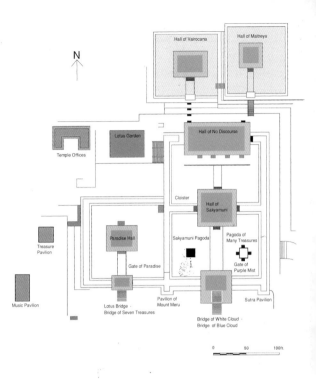

A ground plan of Bulguksa temple (right).

including the foundations, staircases, platforms and several pagodas date from that time, but the wooden edifices date from 1973 when the temple was completely restored.

Two large stone balustraded staircases that were constructed without mortar dominate the temples fasade. The one on the right comprises a lower flight of steps called *Baegungyo* (Bridge of White Clouds) and an upper flight of steps called *Cheongungyo* (Bridge of Azure Clouds) and the one on the left, two flights of steps called *Chilbogyo* (Seven Treasures Bridge) and *Yeonhwagyo* (Lotus Bridge). The staircases are called bridges because symbolically they lead from the secular world to *Bulguk*, the Land of the Buddha.

Baegungyo leads to *Jahamun* (Mauve Mist Gate), the main entrance to *Daeungjeon*, the temple's main sanctuary. The other staircase leads to *Anyangmun* (Pure Land Gate), the entrance to *Geungnakjeon*, a secondary sanctum.

The colorful *Daeungjeon* is not Bulguksa's largest building, but it is certainly the most important as it enshrines an image of Sakyamuni, the Historic Buddha. The gilt bronze image made in 1765 is flanked by Dipamkara, the Bodhisattva of the Past, and Maitreya, the Bodhisattva of the Future, and two arhats, or disciples, Ananda and Kasyapa. Ananda, the younger of the two, is a cousin of Sakyamuni and his habitual attendant. Kasyapa is a leading disciple.

The building is decorated with colorful *dancheong* patterns that are not only a reflection of the Buddhist heaven but also an attempt to bring the harmony and unity of the cosmos to earth for easy access by humans. Horned dragons look down from the eaves of the roof.

Dominating the courtyard of *Daeungjeon* hall are two of Korea's most beautiful pagodas: the 8.3-meter-high *Seokgatap* (Pagoda of Sakyamuni) and the 10.5-meter-high *Dabotap* (Many Treasures Pagoda), both built around 756. A mimicry of

Daeungjeon, the main hall of Bulguksa, was rebuilt in 1765. The stone foundations for the building were laid out during the Silla Kingdom (B.C. 57-A.D. 935)

wood construction dominates the motifs of both pagodas. It is recorded that Kim Daeseong had them built for his parents, which is perhaps why the *Seokgatap* is rather masculine and the *Dabotap* feminine. *Seokgatap* is characterized by simplicity and princely dignity whereas *Dabotap* is highly decorative. The simple, three-story *Seokgatap* represents spiritual ascent via the rules put forth by Sakyamuni, Buddhism's historical founder, whereas the more complex *Dabotap* symbolizes the complexity of the world.

Geungnakjeon (Hall of Great Bliss), which is to the left of *Daeungjeon*, enshrines a gilt-bronze

image of Amitabha, the Buddha of the Western Paradise. A masterpiece of Buddhist sculpture, the lovely image is believed to have been made in 1750.

Behind *Daeungjeon* is the temple's largest building, a 34.13-meter-long lecture hall called *Museoljeon*. It is interesting to note that the name literally means no lecture, implying that truth cannot be obtained through lectures. Behind and

Dabotap (the Pagoda of Many Treasures) (left); and *Seokgatap* (the Pagoda of the Historic Buddha) (right).

to the left of this hall is *Birojeon* (Hall of Vairocana), where an imposing gilt-bronze image of Vairocana, the Buddha of All-pervading Light, made during the eighth or ninth century, is enshrined. The mudra, or hand gesture of this image, symbolizes that the multitude and the Buddha are one. To the right of *Birojeon* is *Gwaneumjeon* in which an image of Avalokitesvara, the Bodhisattva of Mercy, is

enshrined. The image was made when the temple was restored.

High up on the mountain behind Bulguksa temple is Seokguram, a man-made stone grotto designed around the worship of a principal statue of Buddha. One of Asia's finest Buddhist grottos, it is a reflection of the application of advanced scientific principles and precise mathematical and architectural concepts, not to mention great technical skills. It is also a testament to the enthusiasm, courage, and

The main hall enshrines a gilt wooden Buddha triad flanked by earthen images of the two disciples of the Historic Buddha.

sacrifice of Korea's early Buddhist monks who risked their lives to make pilgrimages to faraway India to learn firsthand about their religion and its traditions.

This type of cave temple originated in India where two kinds were constructed: *chaitya*, a sanctuary or hall containing a sacred object to be worshipped such as an image of a Buddha or a small stupa; and *vihara*, a monastery or shelter for monks, often with a stupa or niches for images. Grotto temples of the *chaitya* style were popularized in China. Both *chaitya* and *vihara* were created by tunneling in stone mountains and carving on natural rocks.

Seokguram follows the *chaitya* model but it was not created by tunneling; perhaps Korea's granite bedrock precluded the type of tunneling and carving involved in the Indian and Chinese cave temples. Instead, the cave, which is high up on the mountain some 750 meters above sea level, was artificially created using carved granite slabs. Kim Daeseong constructed Seokguram at the same time he built Bulguksa temple and at the time, it was called Seokbulsa, literally Stone Buddha temple. It was designed to guide the Buddhist faithful into the land of the Buddha, to enable them to take a spiritual journey to the realm of nirvana.

Seokguram comprises a rectangular antechamber and a round interior chamber with

One of the miniature statues of seated Bodhisattvas and faithfuls ensconced in the 10 niches on the wall of the main rotunda of Seokguram (below).

The main rotunda of the Seokguram Grotto (previous page).

A legion of bas-relief images of various guardian deities decorate the walls of the antechamber of Seokguram (above).

a domed ceiling connected by a rectangular passageway. The antechamber represents earth and the round chamber, heaven. A large image of a seated Buddha is in the rotunda. It is placed in the rotunda in such a way that the first rays of the sun rising over the East Sea would strike the urna, the jewel in the forehead. Thirty-nine figures from the Buddhist pantheon such as bodhisattvas, arhats and ancient Indian gods are arranged systematically on the walls of the antechamber, corridor and rotunda according to their functions and ranks, giving the impression of having realized the Pure Land of the Buddha in the present world. Most of the images are in high relief.

Chiseled out of a single block of granite, the

3.5-meter-high main Buddha is seated cross-legged on a lotus throne facing the east, eyes closed in quiet meditation, a serene, all-knowing expression on its face. Its features—gentle eyebrows, noble nose, long ears and tightly curled hair—are exquisitely portrayed. The hands are poised in the mudra of calling the earth to witness. An image of power and serenity, it presents Sakyamuni at the moment of

The main rotunda as viewed from the antechamber.

enlightenment. The personification of divine and human natures, an enigmatic combination of masculine strength and feminine beauty, the image represents Buddhist sculpture at the zenith of classical realism. Many art historians consider it to be the most perfect Buddhist statue in the world.

Seokguram and Bulguksa were registered on the UNESCO World Cultural Heritage List in December 1995. At the time, the woodblocks of the *Tripitaka Koreana* and their storage halls at Haeinsa temple, and Jongmyo, the royal

The main Buddha wears a serene, all-knowing smile(top). Buddha is seated in a cross-legged position on a lotus pedestal(middle). Details of the pedestal on which Buddha is seated(below).

ancestral shrine of the Joseon Dynasty, were also added to the list.

The World Cultural Heritage List is part of an international program under which unique and irreplaceable cultural assets located in countries that are signatories to the World Heritage Agreement are recognized for their universal value and registered in an effort to ensure their preservation and maintenance in the interest of all humanity. The World Heritage Committee recognized Bulguksa and Seokguram for being a masterpiece of human creative genius and an outstanding example of an architectural ensemble illustrative of a significant stage in human history.

The inclusion of these Korean cultural assets on the World Cultural Heritage List reflects the world's recognition of the quality and unique character of Korean culture.

Hundreds of granite blocks of various shapes and sizes were assembled to form the cave. The domed ceiling is capped with a round granite plate decorated with a lotus design.

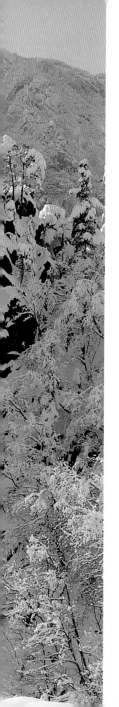

Mt. Seoraksan

Ask a Korean to name the most beautiful place in Korea and the person will no doubt say Mt. Seoraksan, at least nine times out of ten. It is arguably the area most beloved by Koreans.

With high craggy peaks, boulder-strewn streams of crystal clear water, large waterfalls, unusual rock formations, and forests of pine and hardwood, it is certainly one of the most beautiful places Korea has to offer, any time of year.

In Korea spring, summer, autumn and winter have climatic conditions that clearly distinguish them from each other, and no where is this more visible than Mt. Seoraksan. In spring, its slopes become a riot of various shades of pink, purple, white and yellow with the flowering of azaleas, rhododendrons, dogwoods and forsythia. In summer, it is lush with vegetation of every shade of green imaginable and its valleys are filled with the sound of rushing streams and thundering

Snow-covered Mt. Seoraksan.

waterfalls. In autumn, it is a kaleidoscope of brilliant colors as nature changes the foliage to various shades of red, yellow and gold. In winter, it becomes white from its peaks down to its hills and its streams and waterfalls are hushed and still, all is serene.

Unlike most mountains, Mt. Seoraksan does not rise gradually from foothills; it rears up abruptly from the coastal plain, a weathered wall of granite and gneiss topped by serrated peaks that time and the elements have carved into fantastic forms resembling the battlements and towers of a fortress, its ramparts half-veiled in fog. Often, thick mists drift around and between its peaks, blurring their outlines and smudging the forests into images like from an old ink painting.

Indeed, Mt. Seoraksan looks a lot like the classic Korean ink paintings of craggy mountains wreathed in mist. That is because it is part of the southernmost extension of the source of all those paintings – the legendary Mt. Geumgangsan, or Diamond Mountains, most of which lie north of the border between the two halves of Korea.

However, Mt. Seoraksan is not a lone peak. It is actually a series of peaks in the mid-section of the Taebaeksan range that forms the spine of the Korean Peninsula from north to south. It stretches along the east coast of the peninsula and deeply penetrates inland.

The mountain has gone by many names

Mt. Seoraksan in the four seasons.

including Mt. Seolbongsan, Snow Peak Mountain, and Mt. Seolsan, Snow Mountain, but modern Koreans call it Mt. Seoraksan , Snow Rock Mountain. Contrary to these appellations, the mountain is not snow-capped year-round. It got its name because of the outstanding beauty of its winter landscapes and because of the outcroppings of white rocks that give it a snowy appearance when there is no snow. According to an ancient record, the mountain got its name because snow begins to fall there at the time of the harvest moon festival and does not melt completely until the summer solstice. Another record says that it was named for the snow-white boulders that form its peaks.

Daecheongbong, Great Green Peak, is Mt.

Seoraksan's main peak. It rises to 1,708 meters above sea level. It is the highest peak in the Taebaeksan range, and the third highest in South Korea after Mt. Hallasan, a 1,950-meter-high volcanic mountain on the island of Jejudo, and the 1,915-meter-high Mt. Jirisan straddling the border of the three provinces of Jeollanam-do, Jeollabuk-do and Gyeongsangnam-do.

Because of the mountain's scenic beauty and rare flora and fauna, a 163.4-square-kilometer area around *Daecheongbong* was designated a natural monument in 1965. The area was expanded and made a national park in 1970. The park now encompasses 354.6 square kilometers of land and has 28 peaks, 58 valleys, 9 hills, 2 hot springs, 2 mineral springs and 15 grandiose rock formations as well as 12 Buddhist temples and hermitages.

The forests of Mt. Seoraksan are luxurious. They are a mix of deciduous broad-leaved trees with alpine plants and conifers at high elevations near the mountain ridges. They contain a great variety of flora that provide a habitat for many different animals. *Daecheongbong* itself is especially noteworthy as a sanctuary for high-altitude plant life.

There are about 939 different species of plants, 25 species of mammals including the Asian black bear, musk deer, mountain goat, sable, and antelope, 90 species of birds including two rare species of woodpecker, 11 species of reptiles, 9

Sunrise seen from *Daecheongbong*, the tallest peak of Mt. Seoraksan.

species of amphibians, 360 species of insects, and 40 species of freshwater fish living in the national park. Although flora and fauna estimates made by different studies vary considerably, the park is nonetheless an extremely important area from an ecological perspective. In fact, the variety and rarity of the mountain's flora and fauna prompted UNESCO to designate Mt. Seoraksan National Park and some adjacent areas a Biosphere Reserve on August 12, 1982 in order to protect them. In April 1983, a monument was set up in a small park within the national park to commemorate UNESCO's important declaration.

The national park is divided into Outer Seorak and Inner Seorak, or *Oe-Seorak* and *Nae-Seorak*, by the ridges that extend north and south from *Daecheongbong*. Outer Seorak is closest to the sea and Inner Seorak is the farthest inland. Inner Seorak has a more continental type of climate and smooth slopes and thus supports a lush

Pyeongari nancho (Amitostigma gracilis), a perennial of the Orchidaceae family. This variety of orchid grows in rocky, shady places like Seoraksan (left);

Somdari, a type of chrysanthemum (right);

Geumnanghwa, bleeding hearts or Dutchman's breeches (opposite page, left);

Nado-okjamhwa, bear-tongue or wood lily (opposite page, right).

growth of vegetation. Outer Seorak, however, is characterized by a maritime climate and steep slopes, and hence, has less flora and fauna.

The best way to see the park and its many sights is to hike the many trails that crisscross Mt. Seoraksan like a spider's web. But one does not have to hike far to get a taste of what the park has to offer. Many of the main spots of interest are within an hour or two from the main entrance to the park, which is in Outer Seorak, near the main tourist village of Seorak-dong.

Outer Seorak is considered the most scenic area because of its craggy peaks. It is also the most accessible. Sinheungsa temple and its *Gyejoam* hermitage, the *Ulsanbawi* and *Heundeulbawi* rocks, *Biseondae* promontory, and *Biryongpokpo* waterfall are among the most popular sights in Outer Seorak, and they are not far from Seorak-dong. Baekdamsa temple and the *Daeseungpokpo* waterfall are among the most famous sights in Inner Seorak, but they are not easily accessible, requiring considerable hiking.

Sinheungsa temple is the oldest *Seon*(Zen in Japanese) Buddhist temple in Korea, and perhaps even the world. It was originally founded in 653 by *Jajangyulsa*, a revered monk of the ancient Silla Kingdom. The small but historic temple, just a short walk from the park's main entrance, marks the beginning of the trail up the mountain to *Gyejoam*. Located in about as picturesque a location as one could hope to find, *Gyejoam* offers one of the best views of *Daecheongbong*. It is located at the base of *Ulsanbawi* and extends into a natural cave. *Ulsanbawi*, literally meaning Ulsan Rock, is a

Sinheungsa temple, one of the largest temples in the Seoraksan area with more than 40 buildings(left); Mt. Seoraksan in fall(right).

huge hunk of rock that is so named because of a legend that says a god carrying it to Mt. Geumgangsan from Ulsan, a town near the southern end of the peninsula, dropped it when he heard that Mt. Geumgangsan already had 12,000 peaks. It is actually a spectacular outcropping of granite, quartz and mica that rises to an altitude of 873 meters and has a circumference of 4 kilometers. Its six granite peaks and rugged cliffs are spectacular to see. Nearby *Gyejoam* is *Heundeulbawi*, Tottering Rock, a large round boulder sitting so precariously on a cliff that it looks as if it would roll off at the slightest touch. However, it only rocks slightly when pushed and it rocks the same amount whether one person or a group of people pushes

Heundeulbawi,
a tottering rock.

The rugged peaks of *Ulsanbawi rock.*

it. Another trail from Seorak-dong follows a stream up a beautiful, heavily wooded gorge to *Biseondae* promontory, Flying Fairy Peak, a huge, slanting rock over which the stream flows. It is like a giant water slide, and being very slippery, many people do have a slide or two. The 40-meter-high *Biryongpokpo,* or Flying Dragon Waterfall is at the top of a lovely gorge below the Hwachaebong peak. As its name suggests, it looks like a flying dragon. The pool at its base is extremely deep and ideal for swimming.

Inner Seorak is less accessible than Outer

Seorak and has fewer tourist sites but it offers boundless hiking pleasure and memorable scenery. There are numerous trails of various length and difficulty ranging from several hours to several days that lead through Inner Seorak, across the ridges into Outer Seorak.

Baekdamsa temple is one of Inner Seorak's few cultural assets. It is located in the secluded Baekdam Valley, where a stream originating in Gayadong Valley and one from the *Gugokdam* Pool converge. It was built in 647 by *Jajangyulsa*, the revered Silla monk who also founded

Oseam hermitage built in 1643, during the reign of King Injo.

A couple of majestic Seoraksan peaks.

Sinheungsa temple. It was first called Hangyesa temple but later renamed Baekdamsa temple, Temple with One Hundred Pools, because there are 100 pools of water between it and *Daecheongbong*. It is a strenuous 8.5-kilometer hike from the main entrance to the valley and no cars are permitted beyond the entrance. *Daeseungpokpo* waterfall is located at *Jangsudae*. With a height of 88 meters, it is one of the largest and most picturesque waterfalls in Korea. Nearby is the *Ongnyutang* waterfall where, according to legend, a heavenly being fleeing from a monster that attacked it at *Daeseungpokpo* waterfall was saved by a thunderbolt hurled by the gods.

Other popular attractions in Mt. Seoraksan include *Cheonbuldong*, Valley with One Thousand Buddhas, where the elements have shaped rocky outcroppings into shapes that resemble human and animal forms; *Osaek*, Five Color Spring, which is famous for its iron-rich water; and *Gwongeumseong*, a mountaintop fortress. Visiting these or any of the other tourist sites provides an opportunity to soak up the extraordinary beauty of Mt. Seoraksan.

Baegundong Falls.

Korean Artists

G iven the worldwide interest in sports and the extensive media coverage given them, many people may be familiar with Korean golf sensation Park Seri and Los Angeles Dodgers' ace pitcher Park Chanho. However, it is in the field of music and the arts that Koreans have contributed the greatest to world culture.

Violinist Sarah Chang is recognized the world over as one of classical music's most captivating and gifted artists. She first astounded the music world by appearing as a surprise guest performer with the New York Philharmonic Orchestra under the baton of Zubin Mehta. She was eight years old at the time and had just played for Mehta two days earlier when he was so impressed that he immediately asked her to do the performance.

Since that eventful debut she has performed in the music capitals of Asia, Europe and the Americas and collaborated with nearly every major orchestra and with many of the world's

Chung Myungwhun, a world-renowned pianist and conductor.

most esteemed conductors. She has reached an even wider audience through her many television appearances, including several concert broadcasts, and her best-selling recordings.

Her first album, *Debut*, was recorded when she was nine, using a quarter-sized violin. Released in September 1992 to exceptional acclaim, it quickly reached the Billboard's chart of classical bestsellers. She has since released a handful of recordings, the most recent in March 1998. In recognition of her recordings, she was awarded a special 1993 Gramophone award as "Young Artist of the Year." In 1993, she received the German "Echo" Schallplattenpreis and the

Sara Chang, a child prodigy violinist, made her debut when she was eight, playing with the New York Philharmonic Orchestra under the baton of Zubin Mehta.

Royal Philharmonic Society of Music's "Debut" award and in 1994, the "Newcomer of the Year" prize at the International Classical Music Awards. Prior to those honors, she was presented the Nanp'a award, Korea's highest honor for a musical artist, in May 1991, and in May 1992, she became the youngest person to ever be awarded the Avery Fisher Career grant.

Another outstanding Korean violinist who has long wowed music lovers around the world is Chung Kyungwha. For more than 25 years, she has been one of the most sought-after musicians on the international stage, earning recognition as a performing artist of the very highest stature. The *Sunday Times* of London, the city where she resides with her family, has called her one of the most important contributors to the British cultural scene.

She left Korea at the age of 12 to study at the Juilliard School of Music in New York. After winning the Leventritt competition in 1967, she embarked upon her performing career in North America, appearing with many of the finest orchestras. She made her European debut in 1970 at the Royal Festival Hall playing Tchaikovsky with André Previn and the London Symphony Orchestra. Her performance was so outstanding that they immediately booked her for three more London concerts, a tour of Japan and a television appearance. Engagements with the London

Philharmonic, Berlin Philharmonic and Cleveland Orchestra followed and from then on her international career soared.

Since that time she has appeared in recital and with virtually all of the major orchestras and conductors throughout North America, Europe, and Asia. Although she now restricts her performances to no more than 60 a year in order to devote more time to her family, she used to perform nearly 120 concerts each season. She has made numerous recordings and has earned a number of awards including a coveted Gramophone Award.

Chamber music plays a very important part in Chung's performing life as she often performs and records with her brother Chung Myung-whun, a pianist and conductor, and her sister Chung Myungwha, a world-renowned cellist. The Chung Trio, as the three are called, has been honored with the title Honorary Ambassador of the United Nations Drug Control Program.

Cellist Chung Myungwha graduated from Julliard and won first place in the cello division at the Geneva International Competition in 1971. She has since performed with the London Royal Philharmonic, the Berlin Radio Symphony and many other orchestras.

The Principal Conductor of the Orchestra of the Accademia Nazionale di Santa Cecilia and Music Director of the Asia Philharmonic Orchestra, Chung Myungwhun began his

Sisters Chung Kyung-wha, violinist, and Chung Myungwha, cellist.

musical studies as a pianist and made his debut with the Seoul Philharmonic at the age of seven. He studied piano and conducting at the Mannes School of Music in New York. After winning second prize at the 1974 Tchaikovsky Competition in Moscow for piano, he went on to complete his conducting studies at Juilliard. In 1978, he became an assistant to the conductor of the Los Angeles Philharmonic and in 1980, he was named an associate conductor. His career began to soar with his appointment in 1984 to Music Director and Principal Conductor of the Saarbrü ken Radio Symphony Orchestra, which he held until 1990.

He has conducted many prominent European

orchestras, including the Berlin Philharmonic, Vienna Philharmonic, Munich Philharmonic, Orchestre National de France, Orchestre de Paris, La Scala Orchestra and Concertgebouw. In North America he has made guest appearances with the New York Philharmonic, Philadelphia Orchestra, Chicago Symphony, Cleveland Orchestra and Boston Symphony. He toured Asia in 1995 with the Philharmonia Orchestra and in 1996 with the London Symphony Orchestra.

For the last dozen or so years, he has devoted his attention to opera. He made his opera debut at the Metropolitan Opera in 1986 and from 1987 to 1992 he was the Principal Guest Conductor of the Teatro Comunale in Florence, during which time he was awarded the Premio Abbiati by Italian critics in 1989 and the following year was awarded the Arturo Toscanini prize. He was the Music Director of the Opéra de Paris-Bastille from 1989 to 1994 and for his outstanding work he was named "Artist of the Year" by the Association of French Theatre and Music Critics in 1991, and the French government awarded him the Légion d'Honneur in 1992 for his contribution to French opera.

In 1995, the United Nations Educational, Scientific and Cultural Organization (UNESCO) named him its "Man of the Year." In 1996, he received the highest cultural award of the Korean government for his contributions to

World acclaimed soprano Sumi Jo, active mostly on European opera stages, was discovered by the legendary conductor Herbert von Karajan.

Korean music. Chung now serves as Honorary Cultural Ambassador for Korea, the first in the Korean government's history.

Soprano Sumi Jo was discovered by the world-famous conductor Herbert von Karajan, who praised her as having a "god-given voice." Since her debut on the Italian stage in 1986, singing Gilda in Verdi's "Rigoletto" with Karajan directing, she has performed around the world and in all the major opera houses. She has made

Yun Isang was one of Korea's best known musical composers.

many outstanding recordings and in 1993 Italian critics named her "Best Soprano of the Year." A highly versatile singer, she has a vast repertoire of over 30 operas.

Jo went to Rome in 1983 to study voice at the Accademia di Santa Cecilia. In 1985, after finishing her five-year course in just two years, she won the top prize in four singing competitions in Italy.

The late modern classical composer Yun Isang (1917-1995) had an influence that went far beyond Korea's borders. In fact, many credit Yun with having put Korea on the world's musical map with operas and symphonies combining his inspirations from Oriental traditions with techniques of Western music. Although he spent most of his life outside Korea, his oeuvre is characterized by the lively, flexible tone of Korea's traditional music. By integrating the principles of European New Music into his Korean-inspired "main tone technique," he blended Eastern and Western attributes to create a composition style reflecting the Taoist *eum(yin)-yang* concept. He composed over 150 musical works including symphonies and operas, many of them inspired by political developments in Korea.

The son of a poet, Yun began to write music at the age of 14. After studying Western music in Korea, he studied voice, theory, harmony and composition in Japan from 1935 to 1943 when he returned to Korea to teach. In 1955, he won the Seoul City Award which enabled him to travel to Europe for further study. He studied in Paris from 1956 to 1957 and in Berlin from 1958 to 1959. He eventually settled in Germany and taught music composition at Berlin Hochschule für Musik from 1970 until his retirement in 1985. In 1987, the then West German government awarded him its highest state medal, and to celebrate his 75th birthday in 1992, concerts featuring his music were held in several cities in Germany as well as in Switzerland, the Netherlands, Japan and North Korea.

Another composer, and one which Koreans hold very dear, is Ahn Eaktay (1905-1965) who

Ahn Eaktay, composer of the national anthem and *Korea Fantasia*, was better known overseas as a conductor, who found his niche in Germany during World War II.

wrote the music for Korea's national anthem, *"Aegukga."* However, he is probably better known outside Korea for his *Korea Fantasia*, a long epic piece depicting the glorious feats and ordeals Korea experienced throughout its 5,000-year history that was first performed by the Irish National Symphony in 1938.

Ahn first studied music in Japan, majoring in cello. In 1930, he went to the United States for further study, first in Philadelphia and later in Cincinnati where he also played first chair cello with the Cincinnati Symphony Orchestra. He entered the Franz Liszt Academy of Music in Budapest in 1936. In 1937, he went to Vienna to study under Richard Strauss and that same year he took up the baton as the permanent conductor of the Mallorca Orchestra in Madrid. Thereafter, he served as guest conductor for more than 200 orchestras around the world.

In the field of Korean traditional music, perhaps no individual or group has been more in the international spotlight than Kim Duksoo and his percussion quartet Samulnori. Playing four Korean traditional percussion instruments—an *janggu* or *janggo* (hourglass drum), *buk* (barrel drum), *jing* (large gong) and *kkwaenggwari*(small gong)— the quartet combines traditional rhythmic constructs derived from the wandering bands of old with shamanistic ceremonies and modern compositions to create a unique musical experience that is both ancient and contemporary, energizing and mesmerizing, vigorous and athletic.

Founded in 1978, the quartet opened a new era in Korean traditional music and its staging and spawned a new genre of music that has come to be called *Samulnori. Samulnori* gave its first overseas performance in 1982 and since that time it has performed in concert on all the major continents. In addition, the quartet has performed and recorded with folk bands and percussion groups of various countries as well as with orchestras, classical and jazz ensembles, and big name jazz artists such as Pushkin, Steve Gadd and Nexus.

Surprisingly, Paik Namjune, the Korean-born artist known the world over as the "father of video art," began his career as a musician and composer studying at the University of Tokyo, the University of Munich, and the Conservatory of Music in Freiburg, Germany. Influenced by the composer John Cage, Paik's interests brought him into contact with an international movement of artists who sought to break down the barriers between high art and everyday life. He began combining music and art, and was attracted to video by the random quality of the television soundtrack. In 1963, he became the first person to exhibit "prepared" television sets. Since that time Paik has influenced contemporary art, video and television with works linking the worlds of art, media, technology, pop culture and the avant garde.

A provocative and prophetic spokesman for new uses of television technology and for the relevance of TV to art, Paik has used television sets in startling constructions such as a cello, a bra, and eyeglasses and has designed installations composed of tele-visions transformed into aquariums and stacked as

Avant-garde video artist and musician Paik Namjune (left) and his work, entitled *MAN ON HORSEBACK*.

pyramids. He has made TV chairs and many versions of TV robots. Many of his works combine fast-paced video clips in montages programmed over a number of television monitors.

Paik's art can be found in museums and private collections around the world. In 1982, the Whitney Museum of American Art honored him with a comprehensive retrospective of videotapes, video sculptures, installations and performances. In 1993, he won the grand prize at the Venice Biennale and that same year the German monthly *Kapitol* named him one of the world's greatest artists. The U.S. cable network Discovery recently featured him and his works in

Poet So Chongju (left), whose poems have been translated into English, German, and Spanish; Novelist Yi Munyol (right), whose novels were translated into many foreign languages and have drawn critical attention.

a documentary.

Although he is not a musician, it is through the medium of the musical that best-selling writer Yi Munyol has most recently come into the international spotlight. *The Last Empress*, a Broadway-style musical based on his 1994 best-selling novel *The Fox Hunt*, opened to rave reviews at the New York State Theater of the Lincoln Center in August 1997 and has since been touring North America. Many of Yi's works have been translated into other languages and have drawn critical attention abroad.

Another writer who has attracted considerable attention in international literary circles is poet So Chongju. Translations of his poems have been published in the United States, Germany, France and Spain.

These people are just a handful of the many brilliant individuals who have contributed significantly to putting Korea on the world's cultural map as well as enhancing the nation's image in the global community. Their remarkable creativity, highly refined artistry and distinguished performances are a source of pride for all Koreans.

Printing Heritage

In the cultural history of the world, the Korean people stand out as having created a brilliant tradition in printing. For example, woodblock printing began in the 8th century in Korea. The world's first metal typeface was developed by the Koreans more than 200 years before Gutenberg in Germany.

Long before the use of letters, human beings used various symbols and signs to communicate and to keep track of records. The engraved symbols and pictures on the surface of stones used by the primitive ancestors of Koreans can be seen in the stone carvings discovered in Cheonjeon-ri, Ulsan. After letters were introduced, transcription greatly enhanced the effectiveness of indirect communication. Engraved in stone or metal, the symbols and letters could withstand the erosion of thousands of years, and rubbings could be taken from them for the education of future generations.

After Buddhism was introduced to Korea in 372 during the Three Kingdoms period,

Korea's printing tradition is the oldest in the world.
The *Daejanggyeong* (Tripitaka Koreana) which was carved from 1236 to 1251 is preserved in *Janggyeongpanjeon* hall at Haeinsa temple.

transcription and engraving in stone or metal became a widespread practice to propagate the teachings of the Buddhist scriptures. The missionary zeal of the believers led to an enormous increase in the production of paper and ink-sticks. Thus, as early as the Three Kingdoms period, Koreans were transferring their knowledge in making paper and ink-sticks to Japan. They were also exporting their products to China, where the paper later came to be well known as *Silla paper, Goryeo paper,* or *Joseon paper,* depending on the different periods in Korea. In short, with the religious fervor of Buddhism providing the impetus, the necessary ingredients for the early development of printing-paper, ink, and the message were well in place during the Three Kingdoms period.

Historical records indicate that woodblock

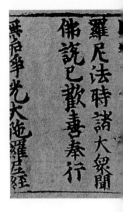

The world's oldest existing woodblocks were used to print *Mugujeonggwang daedaranigyeong* (Pure Light Dharani Sutra).

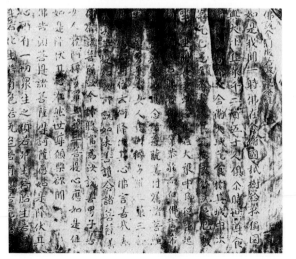

This metal-block of a sutra (Buddhist scripture), produced sometime between the late Unified Silla period and the early Goryeo period, well illustrates the technique in carving blocks that served both as a base for making a rubbed copy and as a prototype for woodblock printing.

罷八部等咸礼佛之
同聲白言我等已
蒙世尊加護福此
咒法及造塔法咸此日
守衛住持讀誦書寫
供養為護一切諸衆生
故於後時參令彼衆
生悉得聞知不堕地
獄及諸悪趣我等為
報如来大恩咸共守護
令廣流通倍重恭敬
如佛无異不令此法命
有壞滅佛言善哉
善哉汝等乃能堅

printing was being practiced in Korea in the
beginning of the 8th century. A Buddhist
scripture printed from woodblocks dating to the
Silla period, was retrieved from Bulguksa temple
in Gyeongju. The title of the scripture is
Mugujeonggwang daedaranigyeong (Pure Light
Dharani Sutra). It is presumed to have been
translated into Chinese characters by a monk
named Mitasan around the year 704. One record
also indicates that it was placed within the stone
pagoda of Hwangboksa temple in 706. Others
place it as the scripture that inspired the
construction of numerous pagodas in Japan.
Since the pagoda at Bulguksa temple from where
the scripture was retrieved was built in 751, the
scripture itself must have been printed well
before that year. Though it is small, the print
reveals the characteristics of early woodblock
printing in Korea, and attests to the lofty heights
in cultural accomplishments that the Korean
people at the time reached. It remains the
world's oldest printed material.

Meanwhile, Choe Chiwon, the great scholar of

the Silla Kingdom, wrote in one of his many books that a collection of Silla poetry had been printed and sent to an envoy of Tang in China. The statement is testimony to the widespread use of printing during the Silla period.

Printing further developed during the Goryeo Dynasty (918-1392). Having adopted Buddhism as the state religion, numerous Buddhist temples were built, and printing was promoted as a way to disseminate Buddhist teachings during the Goryeo Dynasty. Of them, the oldest remaining text is *Bohyeop indaranigyeong*, printed at Chongjisa temple in 1007. It shows the highly refined craftsmanship of Goryeo woodblock printers.

During the reign of Hyeonjong (1010-1031), the printing blocks for *Chojodaejanggyeong* (first trimmed Tripitaka) were carved (1011-1031). Later the blocks for *Sokjanggyeong*, a comprehensive collection of the studies and footnotes on the Tripitaka were also made (1091-1101). The blocks for both works were burned to ashes during the Mongol invasion in 1232. The King ordered them remade, even under the hardships of war, which took place between 1236 and 1251. The resulting masterpieces *Tripitaka Koreana*, have been preserved to this day at Haeinsa temple in Hapcheon-gun, Gyeongsang-nam-do province and are the world's oldest remaining woodblocks for the Tripitaka. They are also the most accurate and comprehensive, used by the Chinese and Japanese as the standard reference in Buddhism studies. Printing flourished in other temples during the Goryeo

A woodblock for the *Tripitaka Koreana* housed at Haeinsa temple.

Dynasty as well, churning out Buddhist scriptures, collections of poetry and essays by monks. Confucian teachings, medical treatises, historical writings, poetry and essays by noted scholars were also carved in wood for printing.

In the *Dongguk-isanggukjip,* the author notes that printing with metal type was already being done in the Goryeo Dynasty (918-1392).

Goryeo Dynasty printing is noted for its invention of metal typeface. With woodblocks alone, the exploding demand for quality printed materials could not be fully met. The clever people of the Goryeo period overcame that challenge by inventing characters cast in metal. The exact date of the invention is difficult to identify. Some argue that it was during the 11th century; others say it was sometime during the 12th. One author writing on woodblocks in 1239 indicated that metal characters were around well before 1232. Furthermore, the famous scholar-official Yi Gyubo (1168-1241) wrote in his masterpiece *Donggukisanggukjip* (Collected Works of Minister Yi of Goryeo) that 28 copies of *Sangjeongyemun* (prescribed ritual texts) were printed with metal characters.

One of Goryeo's early metallograph works,

Baekunhwasangchorok Buljo jikjisimcheyojeol or *Jikjisimgyeong* for short (the Selected Sermons of Buddhist Sages and Seon Masters) printed at Heungdeoksa temple in Cheongju in 1377, is kept at the French National Library in Paris. The book is proof that metal type was widely used

Jikjisimgyeong was printed with metal type during the Goryeo Dynasty.

during Goryeo. In the book *Goryeosa* (History of Goryeo), it is recorded that in 1392 King Gongyang gave the government office *Seojeokwon* (books and publications center) the responsibility of overseeing all matters related to casting metal types and printing books.

During the Joseon Dynasty (1392-1910), metal, wood, and even ceramic characters were used for printing. Metal types were also called *Juja* (cast characters) and were made of copper, zinc, iron, and other metals. The founder of the Joseon Dynasty, King Taejo, kept alive the operations of Goryeo's *Seojeokwon* . During the time of King Taejong, a separate casting office–*Jujaso* or type casting center– was established (1403). The printed materials consisted largely of books and

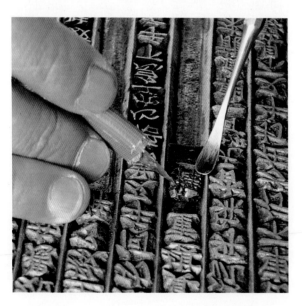

Koreans are studying their printing heritage by recreating the characters used in the *Jikjisimgyeong.*

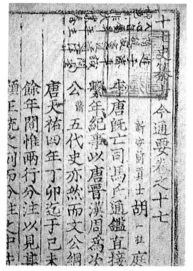

Gyemija, the first metal type made in 1403 during the Joseon Dynasty (left).

Gyeongjaja, made in 1420, corrected the defects of *Gyemija* (right).

documents deemed necessary by the government. They were distributed to the central and local administration, village schools, scholars and officials. For further distribution, woodblock printing was employed, as copies from metal types were limited.

The first set of metal characters made by the *Jujaso* during the Joseon Dynasty was the *Gyemija* characters, named after the year (1403) in which it came out. In 1420, it was refined into the *Gyeongjaja* characters. The third set, the *Gabinja* characters came out in 1434, King Sejong mobilized the efforts of the scholars and engineers of astronomical implements employed at his court to create the set. The result was a set far more exquisite than the previous ones, and it could print twice as many copies as the

Gyeongjaja set. King Sejong also had his scholars and craftsmen develop printing characters for *Hangeul*, the Korean alphabet. The beauty and harmony of the printed Chinese and Korean characters attest to the preeminence of the *Gabinja* among all metal characters that were developed in Korea. Thus, the Joseon court had the set reproduced six times. In 1436, it produced the *Byeongjinja*, named after the year. They were the first soldered characters in the world.

Afterward, numerous other character sets were developed based on various styles of writing; however, most were destroyed or plundered during the *Imjinwaeran* (Japanese invasions of 1592-1598). When they retreated, the invaders took with them countless ceramic

Gabinja, one of the best Korean metal characters, produced in 1434 (left). *Byeongjaja* made in 1516 (right).

artisans and type-casting craftsmen, who later became the seeds for the flowering of printing in Japan. Amid the destruction of the war, it was difficult to secure the raw materials needed to make printing characters. But even then, the soldiers of *Hullyeondogam* (military training command of Joseon) printed books using wooden characters and sold them to raise money for the war efforts. The characters were known as the *Hullyeondogamja*, and they were used until efforts resumed to make metal characters.

King Kwanghaegun, the 15th monarch of Joseon, rebuilt the casting office and renamed it *Jujadogam*, and had it create the *Muoja* characters in 1618. That was followed by the *Hyeonjong sillokja* characters, intended specifically to print the history of King Hyeonjong's reign, as well as a num-

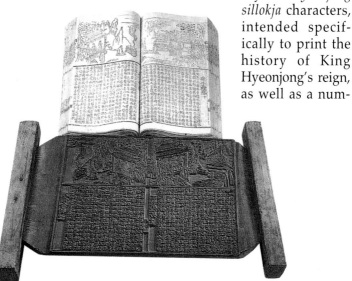

There were virtually no mistakes in the ancient books printed in Korea.
This is a copy of *Seokssiwollyu*, a Buddhist text, and the woodblock used to print it.

ber of other character sets. Altogether, during the Joseon period, some 40 metal character sets were created by the central government offices. Their names typically indicated the year in which they were made, the agency that made them or the individual who provided the prototype character forms.

Needless to say, local administrations, temples, villages and schoolhouses were also active in printing. In the local regions, wooden characters or blocks were largely employed.

Metal typography and printing flourished during the Joseon Dynasty, but the technique of woodblock printing inherited from Goryeo also continued. In early Joseon, Buddhism persevered among the royalty even in spite of the official anti-Buddhism policy of the new dynasty and provided the support for the continued printing of Buddhist scriptures. During King Sejo's time, *Gangyeongdogam*, a special printing office was established to translate and print Buddhist works. The influence of the royal court could be seen in the delicate engraving on the printing blocks.

But the largest portion of woodblock printing during the Joseon period took place at the local government offices, temples, or village schoolhouses. Equipped with the necessary manpower and material resources, temples were particularly active in producing Buddhist scriptures as well as poetry and essay collections and even Confucian writings. They were the professional woodblock printers of the time.

直指心經字
Jikjisimgyeongja

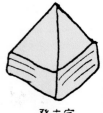

癸未字
Gyemija

Various metal types used in Korea from the Goryeo to the Joseon period.

庚子字
Gyeongjaja

Woodblock printing remained quite popular throughout the Joseon Dynasty, as there was no limit to the number of copies that could be made and the blocks were easy to keep. But as the centuries passed by, the quality declined and the engraving became coarse.

It is noteworthy that misprints are hardly ever found in Korea's ancient books. This, however, is not surprising, since the system did not permit error. As indicated in *Gyeonggukdaejeon* (Grand Code for Managing the Nation) and other historical records, punishment of related workers was severe: for a single error found in an entire volume, everyone, from the top supervisor to the lowest level intern, was caned thirty times; five or more mistakes led to dismissal.

Indeed, the Joseon Dynasty developed a uniquely rich tradition in printing: for five centuries, the government took the lead in creating metal characters, local entities kept alive the tradition of woodblock printing, and great books of impeccable type were printed. Throughout world history, it is difficult to find a comparable example.

However, these days, Korea is an importer as far as printing and publications are concerned, despite the honor of having been the world's first user of metal type. There is a growing awareness that the glory of the past should be revived.

甲寅字
Gabinja

Traditional Musical Instruments

T here are approximately sixty traditional Korean musical instruments that have been handed down through the generations, each boasting of a long and rich history. They include the *gayageum* (12-string zither) and the *geomungo* (six-string zither), both presumed to have originated before the sixth century; the three string and three bamboo instruments of the Unified Silla Kingdom; court instruments of the Joseon Dynasty; and numerous others that are still being played.

Native or folk instruments played a major role in the development of music in Korea from early civilizations to the Unified Silla Kingdom (668-935). The Three Kingdoms period(57 B.C.-A.D. 668) witnessed the first introduction of Central Asian instruments into the country. This, along with the subsequent import of Chinese

Korean musical instruments have a long history and tradition. Shown here are musicians performing on court instruments.

Gayageum:
The most representative instrument of Korea.

instruments, most importantly from Tang China during the late Unified Silla period and from Song China during the Goryeo period (918-1392), sparked a significant rise in the number of available instruments. This, in turn, made it possible for musicians to experiment, thereby expanding the scope and depth of local music. With time, Chinese instruments imported during these periods were slowly integrated into local music, and by the time the Joseon Dynasty (1392-1910) was established, they had already become an integral part of Korean music. Traditional Korean instruments can be broadly divided into three groups: string, wind, and percussion instruments. Based on their function, they can further be divided into native (Hyang), Tang (of Chinese origin), and court ceremonial instruments.

STRING INSTRUMENTS
1. Native Instruments

Gayageum (12-string zither): The *gayageum* is the most representative instrument of Korea. Its origin can be traced back to the Kingdom of Gaya in the sixth century, when the Silla Kingdom was ruled by King Jinheung. However, the actual production of the first *gayageum* is presumed to have been much earlier. The instrument is constructed with 12 strings supported by 12 moveable bridges. The *gayageum* can be divided into two groups according to the types of music played upon them. The *sanjo gayageum* is used in folk and improvisatory musical pieces such as *sanjo* (solo music with drum accompaniment) and *sinawi* (improvisational ensemble music). The *jeongak gayageum* is used in chamber music such as *Yeongsanhoesang* (mass at the sacred mountain) or to accompany lyric songs.

Geomungo:
An important
Korean
instrument.

Geomungo (six-string zither): Along with the *gayageum, the geomungo* is one of the most important Korean instruments. Instruments that appear to be early, primitive forms of the

geomungo have been discovered inside ancient Goguryeo tombs in various locations. The *geomungo* that is used today is constructed with six strings and 16 frets, and is played with a plectrum. It is used to accompany lyric songs as well as in chamber music and *sanjo* (solo music with drum accompaniment).

Haegeum

2. Tang Instruments
(Instruments of Chinese origin)

Haegeum (two-string fiddle): Although it was first imported from China, the *haegeum* has since been fully absorbed into the local culture. Today it is popularly used in various genres of Korean music. The instrument is played by inserting a resined bow between the two strings and rubbing it against the strings. It is currently used in *jeongak* (chamber music) and *sanjo* (solo music with drum accompaniment). In particular, the *haegeum* is an indispensable part of *samhyeon yukkak*, the ensemble consisting of string and wind instruments that are used to accompany dance.

Ajaeng (seven-string bowed zither) : The three types of *ajaeng* are the *jeongak ajaeng*, the *sanjo ajaeng*, and the *daejaeng*. The *jeongak ajaeng* is constructed with seven strings and is used in

Ajaeng concert (right).

Tang music such as *Nagyangchun* (Spring in Loyang) and *Boheoja* (Walking in the Void) as well as in native music such as *Yeomillak* (Enjoyment with the People) and *Jeongeup* (A song of Jeongeup city). The *sanjo ajaeng* has eight strings and is used exclusively in folk music such as *sanjo* and *sinawi*. The *daejaeng* is a large *ajaeng* with fifteen strings. While once widely used to play Chinese music during the Goryeo and Joseon Dynasty, the *daejaeng* is no longer in use.

3. Court Ceremonial Instruments

Geum (seven-stringed zither): The *Geum* has seven strings and a base with thirteen marks inlaid with mother-of-pearl, which mark the

Daegeum (left) and *sogeum* (right).

place where to press down on the string. Used exclusively in court music ensembles during the Joseon Dynasty, the instrument is no longer used.

Seul (twenty-five string zither): This instrument has twenty five strings with 25 bridges. Along with the *geum*, the *seul* was used exclusively in court music ensembles and like the former is no longer played.

4. Other Instruments

Yanggeum (dulcimer): A European instrument that was imported from China during the 18th century, the *yanggeum* has 14 quadruple brass strings stretched over and under two brass bridges. The instrument is played by tapping the strings with a small bamboo stick.

WIND INSTRUMENTS
1. Native Instruments

Daegeum (large transverse flute): The *daegeum* is one of three bamboo wind instruments of the Unified Silla period. The type used during that period was the *jeongak daegeum*. Another type currently used is the *sanjo daegeum*. The *jeongak daegeum* has 13 holes and is typically used for chamber music and song accompaniment. While similar to the *jeongak daegeum* in overall construction, the *sanjo daegeum* is slightly smaller in size and shorter in length. The two types of daegeum differ in their application as well: *sanjo daegeum* is used in *sanjo* (solo music with drum accompaniment) and *sinawi* (improvisational ensemble music) or to accompany folk songs and dance. The two types show a variation in pitch of a minor third when played with three holes.

Hyangpiri

Sogeum (small flute): The *sogeum* is one of the three bamboo instruments along with the *daegeum* (large flute) and the *junggeum* (medium-sized flute). While popularly used until the Joseon Dynasty, there are no remaining relics or prototypes to verify the exact shape of the instrument. A model of the *sogeum* was reconstructed based on existing documents, and this is the type that is currently being used.

Hyangpiri (Korean cylindrical oboe) : The *hyangpiri* has seven finger holes and is used to perform *jeongak* such as *Yeongsanhoesang* and *Jeongeup*, and folk music including *sanjo* (solo music with percussion accompaniment) and wind orchestration.

Chojeok (grass flute) : Made from blades of grass, the *chojeok* was widely popular among the common folk of Korea.

2. Tang Instruments (instruments of Chinese origin)

Dangpiri (Chinese oboe) : Shorter than *hyangpiri* but with a thicker cylinder, the current version of *dangpiri* has eight holes and is typically used to perform Chinese music.

Tungso (vertical flute): The two types of *tungso* are the *jeongak tungso* and the folk *tungso*. The *jeongak tungso* has nine holes and while widely popular until the Joseon Dynasty, it is no longer used. The folk *tungso* has five holes in all, one in the back, and

Tungso (left) and *dangpiri* (right).

Taepyeongso

Yak (left)
and jeok.(right).

Danso

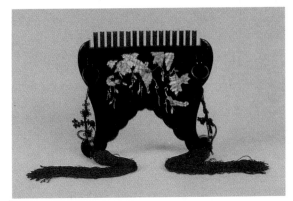

So

four in the front. One has a reed membrane. The instrument is used in *sinawi* (improvisational ensemble music), *sanjo* (solo music with drum accompaniment) and the *Bukcheong* lion dance.

Taepyeongso (conical oboe): The *taepyeongso* was imported from China in the late fourteenth century during the late Goryeo or early Joseon Dynasty. With eight finger holes, the instrument is played by inserting a reed in the blowhole. It is most widely used in *nongak* (farmers music).

3. Court Ceremonial Instruments

Saeng (mouth organ), ***U*** (large mouth organ), and ***Hwa*** (small mouth organ): The three mouth organs are similar in construction and only differ in the number of pipes. The *saeng* has 17 pipes, the *hwa* has 13, and the *u*, the largest, has 36. The only one still in use is the *saeng* used to perform both Chinese and native music.

So (panpipes): The three types are the 12-pipe,

the 16-pipe, and the 24-pipe. The only one still being used in Korea is the 16-piped version, exclusively in court ceremonial music.

Hun (globular flute): The *hun* is created from baked clay and has five holes in all. It is used exclusively in *Munmyo Jeryeak* (ritual music performed at Confucian shrines).

Ji (flute with mouthpiece): The *Ji* has five finger holes in all, one in the back and four in front. The intervals between the holes are irregular. The instrument is used exclusively in court ceremonial music.

Yak (small-notched flute): Played vertically, the *yak* has three finger holes and is used in court music.

Jeok (flute): Played vertically, the *jeok* has one

blowhole and six finger holes and is used in court ceremonial music.

4. Other Instruments

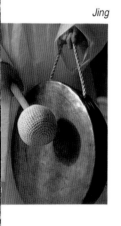
Jing

Danso (vertical flute): First played during the late Joseon Dynasty, the *danso* has five finger holes. It is used in chamber music such as *Yeongsanhoesang* and also for solo perfomances.

Sepiri (slender cylind-rical oboe): The *sepiri* is a slenderized version of the *hyangpiri* and has less volume. The instrument is used in orchestral music where the string section provides the core performance. It is also used in chamber ensemble music such as *Yeongsanhoesang* and in lyric songs, *gasa* (vernacular narrative verse), and *sijo* (short lyric songs).

PERCUSSION INSTRUMENTS
1. Native Instruments

Jing (large gong): Made from brass and played with a mallet wrapped in cloth, the *jing* was originally used in military music. Currently, it is widely used in a variety of music including *chwita* (band music for royal processions), *nongak*, *musok* music (shaman ritual music), and Buddhist music.

Kkwaenggwari

Kkwaenggwari (small gong or hand gong): Similar to the *jing* in its form and construction, the *kkwaenggwari* is smaller in size. Unlike the *jing*, it is played with a small unwrapped mallet and therefore creates a much sharper and high-pitched sound. The instrument is used in *nongak* and *musok* music (shaman ritual music).

Soribuk

Pungmulbuk(folk drum): This is mostly used in *nong-ak* and unlike the *janggo* or *janggu,* (hourglass drum), the materials used on both drumheads are identical.

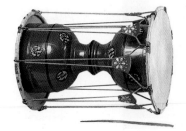

Janggo

The instrument is played by striking the drumheads with a stick made from hard wood.

Soribuk (vocal accompaniment drum): A modified version of the *pungmulbuk*, the *soribuk* is similar to the former in its shape and construction. However, the two differ in that the *soribuk* has tiny metal tacks embedded around the rim of both drumheads. It is mostly used to accompany *pansori* (dramatic narrative singing).

Pungmul Janggo (folk hourglass drum): The *pungmul janggo* has a wooden body with two drumheads made of hide. The instrument is played by striking the drum-heads with two sticks, one in each hand. It is mostly used in *nongak* and also as accompaniment to folk songs and *japga* (folk ballads).

Pungmul janggo, buk, sogo, kkwaenggwari, jing.

bak

2. Tang Instruments
(instruments of Chinese origin)

Bak (clapper): The *bak* is constructed of six wooden slats which are spread apart and then struck together, creating a clapping sound. The instrument was used to perform Chinese music during the Goryeo Dynasty, in court ceremonial music during the early Joseon Dynasty, and then in native music during the mid-Joseon Dynasty. It is used today for *Munmyo Jeryeak* (ritual music performed at Confucian shrines) and court orchestral music and dance accompaniment.

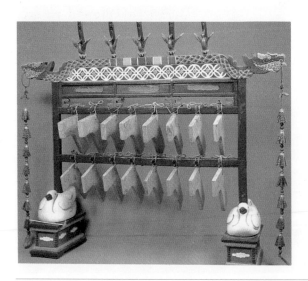

Pyeongyeong

Janggo or *janggu* (hourglass drum): According to existing documents, the *jeongak janggo* has been used since the Goryeo Dynasty. It has a wooden body and is widely used in both Chinese and native music.

3. Court Instruments

Pyeonjong (bronze bells) and *Teukjong* (single bronze bell): The *pyeonjong* is constructed of two rows with eight bells in each row. All the bells are identical in size and only differ in their thickness. The bells are played by striking them with a horn-tipped mallet held in the right hand. The instrument was first imported from Song China during the Goryeo Dynasty. The first domestic production of the *pyeonjong* was under King Sejong during the Joseon Dynasty. Today, it is used in both native and Chinese court music. The *teukjong* has a single bronze bell and is used exclusively in court ceremonial music.

Chuk

Pyeongyeong (stone chimes) and *Teukgyeong* (single stone chime): The *Pyeongyeong* is constructed of two rows with eight L-shaped stones in each row. Imported from China as a

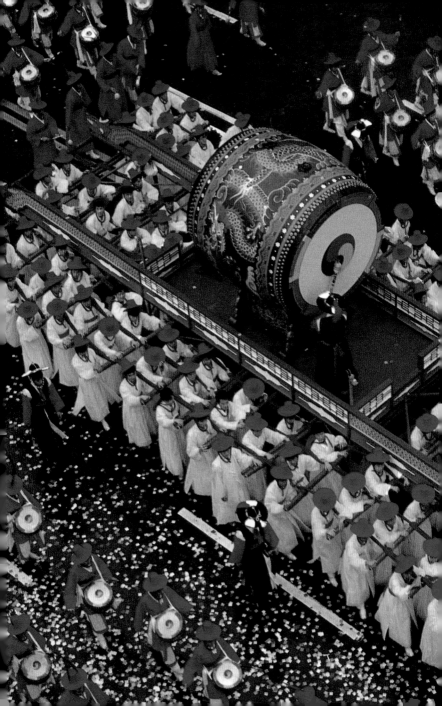

court instrument with the *Pyeongyeong* during the Goryeo Dynasty, the *Pyeongyeong* was first produced domestically under King Sejong during the Joseon Dynasty. Its uses are identical to the *pyeonjong*. The *teukgyeong* is a single L-shaped stone and is used exclusively in court ceremonial music.

Chuk (percussion instrument with a square wooden box and mallet): The *chuk* is one of the instruments used to signal the beginning of a performance. Imported from Song China during the Goryeo Dynasty, it is today used exclusively in ritual music performed at the Confucian and Royal Ancestor Shrine ceremonies.

Eo (tiger-shaped wooden instrument): The *eo* is a tiger-shaped wooden instrument with 27 saw-toothed ridges on its back. The instrument is played by scraping the ridges with a bamboo stick. It is used to signal the end of a performance and is currently used in ritual music performed at Confucian shrines.

A drum processional performed at the 1988 Seoul Olympics.

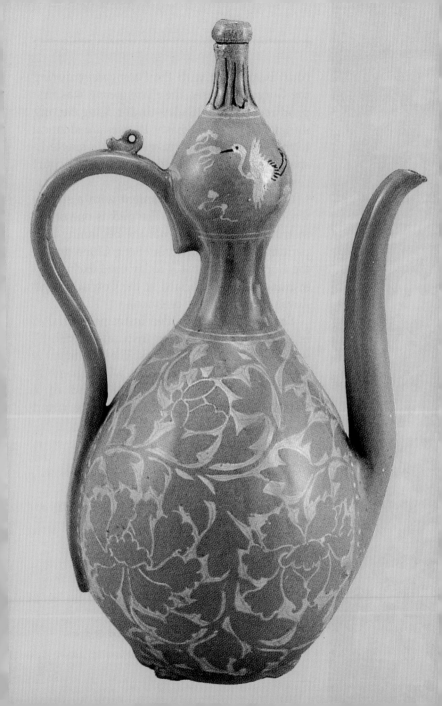

Pottery

Korea boasts a virtually unexcelled cultural tradition of pottery. Deep-rooted in the nation's long history, Korean ceramics are world-renowned. In turn, ceramics have greatly influenced the lifestyle of the Korean people.

Pottery includes earthenware, ceramic ware, stoneware, and porcelain. Historical studies suggest that man first started making earthenware in approximately 10,000 to 6,000 B.C. The oldest kind of Korean earthenware found thus far dates back to 6,000 to 5,000 B.C.

Korea's earliest earthenware was made by firing clay at a temperature of 600 to 800 degrees centigrade or sometime even 1,000 degrees centigrade. The oldest earthenware included those that were just dried without firing. This type of earthenware was only made for a certain period of time. Later on, as man's ingenuity increased, not only was the way of kneading clay improved, but kilns also began to be built that could withstand the heat needed for firing.

Ceramics are produced by firing clay at a

This gourd-shaped vase, National Treasure No.116, is one of the most famous celadon pieces of the Goryeo Dynasty.

temperature ranging from 900 to 1,000 degrees centigrade, which is then glazed. This process includes oxidization that turns the color of e a r t h e n w a r e yellow, brown or red, and celadons and porcelains into yellow or brown.

Stoneware is fired in a kiln whose temperature exceeds 1,100 degrees centigrade. In this process, oxygen is limited to a minimum. Some stoneware is coated with either natural glaze or artificial glaze. This method of firing transforms the color of earthenware into grey, greyish and bluish-black, that of celadon into beautiful greenish-blue, and that of porcelain into mystic light blue. Porcelain is ceramic ware that is made of very pure white clay. It is shaped and glazed with feldspar before being fired at 1,300 to 1,350 degrees centigrade. For that reason porcelain is translucent.

Koreans began to make porcelain in the Neolithic era (7,000 to 8,000 years ago). In the Three Kingdoms period (57 B.C.-A.D. 668), Koreans produced much more refined versions of earthenware that were fired at a very high temperature. Of exceptionally high quality were Silla and Kaya earthenware that was fired at over

1,200 degrees centigrade. The surface of this earthenware is greyish-blue and is extremely sturdy, almost like iron.

With the beginning of the Unified Silla era (668-935), the ground was laid for producing ceramic ware. Potters soon took to making celadon in earnest and eventually some white porcelain. In the Goryeo era (918-1392), the art of making celadon developed greatly, and celadon of extremely high quality was produced.

In addition to Goryeo celadon, other kinds of pottery including iron-glazed and black-glazed pottery were also produced.

The unique, exquisite color of celadon,

Earthenware found in
an old tomb from the Gaya Kingdom.

obtained through an arcane method of firing with reduced oxygen, first appeared in the 11th century and was subsequently further refined. In the 12th century, pure celadon emerged as the most sophisticated Goryeo celadon, and was used mainly by aristocratic households and Buddhist temples.

Goryeo pottery reached its peak in the first half of the 12th century. During the reign of King Injong (r.1122-1146), the firing method further advanced to produce celadon whose almost mystic bluish or gray-green color, often described as 'king-fisher green', defied comparison. The subsequent reign of King Uijong (1146-1170) saw remarkable advance in the technique of inlaying and drawing designs on celadon. In short, Goryeo celadon is widely acclaimed as the best

Goryeo celadon
1. Celadon vase, mid-Goryeo era.
2. Celadon cup.
3. Celadon incense burner,early 12th century.
4. Celadon pillow with two lions.
5. Celadon tile.

1

2

3

4

5

and finest type of pottery for its subdued yet clear, high-spirited bluish-green color, its graceful, flowing curves, and its vivacious shape. Furthermore, the celadon, with its poetic inlaid designs and especially its inlaid copper whose color is artfully transformed to look red, the first technique of its kind ever known in the world, represents the apex of Goryeo pottery.

The 13th century Mongol invasion of Goryeo brought a decline in pottery. As a result, the color, shape and decorative designs of celadon items changed. Celadon pieces took on a mostly dark greenish and opaque glaze and lost much of their graceful shape. Inlaid patterns became rough and were often omitted. Thus the quality to Korean pottery had climaxed with Goryeo celadons as the Joseon era (1392-1910) began to unfold.

Joseon ceramics consisted of two major categories: a type of stoneware called *buncheong* pottery and white porcelain. A product of the early period of the Joseon era, *buncheong* pottery, made for wider use by the masses, is expressive of indigenous Korean folk art. During the period from the final years of the Goryeo era to the early years of Joseon, celadon gave way to *buncheong* pottery on which designs were inlaid, stamped, or painted with iron pigment, or scratched into the slip coating. The glaze on *buncheong* pottery is light blue, and their shapes differ from celadon.

In the period from the late 13th century through the 15th century, Joseon white porcelain, a variation of celadon and Goryeo white porcelain, was also produced. In addition, a new version of Joseon porcelain that was quite different from traditional Goryeo pottery was produced. Thus, together with Goryeo ceramics, *buncheong* pottery and the new version of Joseon white porcelain, formed the mainstream of Korean pottery through the 16th century.

Buncheong pottery is different in both shape and other characteristics from white porcelain. *Buncheong* pottery varies greatly in its decorative designs, whereas white porcelain is made entirely of white clay and has no decorative designs on it. Overall, the color of Joseon pottery tended to be white.

The Japanese invasions of the Korean Peninsula in the late 16th century dealt a major

Buncheong pottery.

Buncheong pottery,
15th century,
National Treasure No.179.

White porcelain jar,
early Joseon era (mid -15th century),
National Treasure No. 219.

White celadon, early Joseon era.

White celadon pencil case.

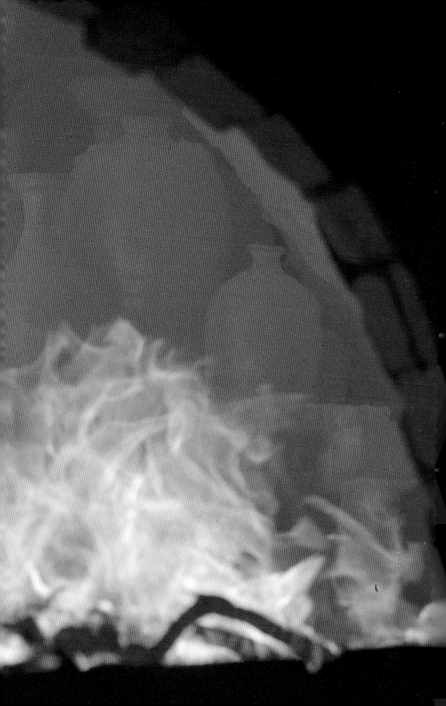

blow to Korean pottery. During the invasions, numerous kilns were destroyed, and many Korean potters were taken as captives to Japan. All this caused a major setback to the development of Korean pottery, while these captured Korean potters eventually gave a major boost to the rise of the ceramics industry in southern Japan. In particular, the devastation by the Japanese invaders virtually brought an end to the production of *buncheong* ceramics, one of the two principal pottery styles of the Joseon period.

From the first year (1392) of the reign of King Taejo to the 27th year (1649) of the reign of King Injo of the Joseon era, *buncheong* and white porcelain constituted the main stream of Korean pottery, although *buncheong* became increasingly dominant during the 15th century. However, beginning in the second half of the 16th century, the production of *buncheong* pottery dwindled and virtually ceased before the 1592-1598 Japanese invasions took place. No *buncheong* ware was produced after the Japanese invasions. *Buncheong* basically resembles Goryeo celadons in its form and shape. Yet, characteristically, *buncheong* exhibits sprightly, daring and often humorous and yet gracious lines.

The shade of high-quality white porcelain produced in the earlier Joseon period is pale blue, reminiscent of the clear skies

White porcelain peach-shaped ink container.

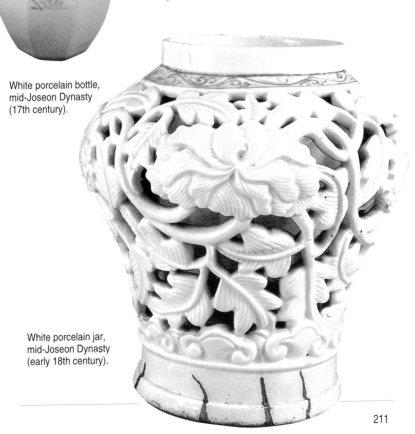

shortly after daybreak following a night of snowfall. The serene, dignified beauty of a white porcelain with no decorative design on it is virtually unrivalled.

This kind of white porcelain reached its heyday in the late period of the Joseon Dynasty, although similar types of white porcelain appeared in some quantities in the early period of the same dynasty.

During the reign of King Sejong (r.1418-1450),

White porcelain bottle, mid-Joseon Dynasty (17th century).

White porcelain jar, mid-Joseon Dynasty (early 18th century).

white porcelain with underglaze designs in cobalt blue was produced, though the quantity of such porcelain was relatively limited. Beginning in the second half of the 15th century, Korean potters produced white porcelain with underglaze designs in ferrous iron oxide. By the mid-17th century, the underglaze designs on such porcelains became more simplified and stylized, mostly depicting plants and flowers, such as chrysanthemums, as well as dragons. All these designs elicit the aesthetic beauty that is typically Korean.

This white porcelain underwent a major change in shape and design during the middle period of the Joseon Dynasty, more specifically from 1651, the second year of King Hyojong's reign, to 1751, the 27th year of King Yeongjo's reign-a period that followed the Japanese invasions of the Korean Peninsula (1592-1598) and the Manchu incursions into Joseon (1627 and 1636-1637).

White porcelain ware produced in that period became increasingly pure white in color and took on flat sides. The underglaze designs on the porcelain became less elaborate and more impressionistic in perfect harmony with both the color and shape of the porcelain. Much of the white porcelain, including flatsided jars, produced in the period was particularly noted

White porcelain ink container (19th century).

White porcelain ink container, late 18th century.

for their luminous whiteness; hence they were known as 'snow-white porcelains.'

Some of the white porcelain also produced during that period is especially famous for their paintings of orchid designs emphasizing their unadorned beauty. In the middle to later period of the 15th century, there appeared white porcelain that exhibited the patterns of stylized paintings. These decorative patterns drawn on white porcelain became further simplified, accentuating their thematic expression in a unique manner.

In the period from 1752, the 28th year of the reign of King Yeongjo, through the end of the 19th century, the final period of the Joseon Dynasty, even greater variety of pottery was produced. However, as imperial Japan began to

White porcelain dish, late Joseon Dynasty (late 18th century).

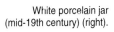

White porcelain jar (mid-19th century) (right).

make increasingly overt attempts to occupy the Korean Peninsula in the late 19th century, a massive quantity of Japanese pottery products flooded the Korean market. Subsequently, the capital-rich Japanese set up large-scale pottery factories, causing the Korean pottery craft to decline rapidly.

Ceramic products mass-produced by the Japanese in Korea consisted mostly of artless porcelain pieces manufactured with machines, in sharp contrast with Korean ceramics that had been handmade and fired in traditional kilns. Nevertheless, Korean potters continued to produce fairly large quantities of traditional jars, such as those used to store drinking water, soy sauce, or *kimchi*, Korea's traditional pickled

Today, Korean potters make traditional jars, used to store drinking water, soy sauce, or *kimchi*.

Recreating the pottery of their forefathers, Koreans continue to produce beautiful items.

vegetable dish.

Today, Korean potters are making enormous efforts to recreate traditional pottery of highly artistic quality through kilns which have been rebuilt in the country side. The most notable kiln sites include Haenam-gun, Jeollanam-do province, and Gwangju-gun and Icheon-gun, Gyeonggi-do province.

Dancheong
Decorative Coloring Used on Buildings

The use of *dancheong* in Korea dates back many centuries, and the skillful techniques developed long ago are still preserved today. *Dancheong* refers to Korean-style decorative coloring used on buildings or other items to convey beauty and majesty, and is done by applying various patterns and paintings in certain areas. Five basic colors are used: red, blue, yellow, black and white.

In addition to its decorative function, *dancheong* was applied for practical reasons as well. It was used to prolong the life of the building and conceal the crudeness of the quality of the material used, while emphasizing the characteristics and the grade or ranks that the building or object possessed. *Dancheong* also provided both a sense of conformity to certain traditions and diversity within the tradition.

Ordinarily *dancheong* refers to the painting of buildings constructed of wood. Coloring of other buildings or objects may be found as well,

Dancheong is a highly developed art in Korea. *Dancheong* of Hwacomsa temple in Gurye, Jeollanam-do province.

adding majesty to a stone building, structural statues or artifacts.

Due to the absence of buildings that date from ancient times, the history of Korean *dancheong* can only be traced via murals in old tombs during the Three Kingdoms period (57 B.C.-A.D. 668). Particularly, in murals of old tombs from the Goguryeo Kingdom (37 B.C.-A.D. 668), there remain diverse colored patterns which show the appearance of *dancheong* and architectural characteristics of that period. Along with those murals, colored pictures and lacquerwork excavated from tombs also show the elements of *dancheong*.

According to historical records of the Three Kingdoms, only nobility with the rank of *seonggol* (those in the royal family qualified to be king) could use the five colors during the ancient Silla Kingdom (57 B.C.-A.D. 668). Unfortunately, no building decorated with *dancheong* from that era remains today. Only through evidence from architectural remains excavated in Gyeongju, the capital of the Silla Kingdom, can it be deduced that *dancheong* during that period was quite delicate and beautiful.

In the Gaoli tujing (*Goryeodogyeong*, Illustrated Account of Goryeo), written in the 12th century by the Chinese scholar Xu Jing(*Seogeung*), it is noted that Goryeo people enjoyed building royal palaces. According to the text, the structure of the places where the king stayed was constructed with round pillars and a square headpiece. The

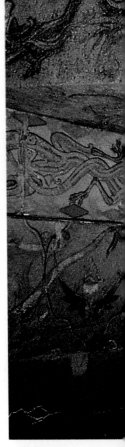

In murals of old tombs from the Goguryeo Kingdom, diverse colored patterns show the early appearance of *dancheong*.

ridge of the roof was colorfully decorated and its configurational structure appeared as if it were about to ascend to the sky. This description suggests the size and majesty of the palace of the Goryeo Dynasty (918-1392), which existed around the 12th century. Xu Jing's book also included a description of the luxurious *dancheong* work, stating that "the handrail was painted in red and decorated with vine-flowers; the coloring was very strong, yet gorgeous, thereby

making the palace stand out among other royal palaces."

Buildings from the Goryeo Dynasty that remain standing today exhibit bright and soft coloring and the *dancheong* lining shows that the *dancheong* techniques used during the Three Kingdoms period were further improved during the Goryeo Dynasty.

During the Joseon Dynasty (1392-1910), Korean *dancheong* work was further developed and diversified. The general characteristics of *dancheong* during that period were a more expressive style and featured a complex unit pattern and decorative composition, along with more luxurious coloring.

There were a number of different types of *dancheong*; even in one particular building, patterns might be differentiated according to the part of the building they were located in. Nevertheless, *dancheong* patterns were systemized in consistent order. The system of patterns was categorized into four different types based on the structural characteristics and positions within the decorative composition. These four types included *morucho, byeoljihwa, bidanmuni* and *dandongmuni.*

Morucho, also called *meoricho,* was a pattern used in painting both ends of supporting beams (such as the ridge of a roof) or corners of a building (such as the tip of eaves). Although the pattern of *morucho* differed based on the era and the building, its basic patterns consisted of a

The delicate and beautiful colors of *dancheong* give it majesty (left).

Dancheong of Baegyangsa temple.

green flower, water lily, pomegranate, bubble, and *whi* (feather), although it should be noted that the whi pattern was not featured in Goryeo era *dancheong*. Using one sample pattern, *morucho* was repeatedly used in all the same parts of a building. Naturally, it occupied the largest amount of space and was most noticeable. *Morucho* was therefore the basic *dancheong* pattern used in almost all types of buildings. During the 18th and 19th centuries, *morucho* developed quite diverse styles, showing the vivid characteristics of Korean *dancheong* technique.

Byeoljihwa refers to decorative painting that utilized a storytelling technique and occupied the gap between two *morucho*. It differed based on the characteristics of the building, and was not used in palace construction; instead, it was most often employed in the construction of temples.

The content of *Byeoljihwa* consisted of auspicious animals (such as dragons, horses, lions, and cranes), the *sagunja* ("the Four Gentlemen" or plum, orchid, chrysanthemum and bamboo), or scenes from Buddhist sutras. Though unrelated to the content of the sutras, the prevailing state of society of the time was also often depicted in temple *byeoljihwa*.

Bidanmuni refers to the diverse coloring of rare and elegant designs or geometric patterns, and

Colorful *dancheong*, where diverse and vivid colors intertwine.

Dancheong patterns were systemized into a set and consistent order. *Dancheong* found on the ceiling of *Cheonguijeong* pavilion.

was used in various parts of the building, particularly in temples, while *dandongmuni* involves the design of a single flower plant or animal, or the application of a single geometric or other pattern in one section.

The colors of *dancheong* reflected the characteristics of the period. During the Goryeo period, parts of a building exposed to outside sunlight, such as pillars, were painted in red, while protruding corners of eaves or ceilings not exposed to sunlight were painted in greenish-blue, so as to enhance to the contrast of brightness and darkness. This application was known as the *sangnok hadan* (green-top, red-bottom) principle.

During the Joseon Dynasty, red, orange, blue, yellow, green, and *seokganju* colors were used profusely. *Seokganju*, also called *juto*, denotes red clay or ocher that yields a dark red or reddish brown pigment typically used for *dancheong* and pottery. This mineral pigment, basically ferric oxide of ferrous sulfate, is noted for its resistance to sunlight, air, water and heat. These were also mixed with white, Chinese ink color and other ingredients to derive various other colors. The colors were separated by insertion of white lines, thereby enhancing the distinctiveness of the pattern's outlining and coloring.

Ordinarily the order of colors used was determined by the characteristics, size, and appearance of the building. Usually, however, two to six colors were used following a set rule. For instance, when a gradual reduction of colors was desired from six colors, colors immediately after the first and immediately before the last colors were eliminated first to achieve a 5-4-3-2 order. Coordination of colors for *dancheong* consisted primarily of juxtaposing different and complementary colors. A technique of alternating a warm with a cold color was used to make the different colors more distinct from each other. Traditionally, typical pigments employed for *dancheong* were derived from *pyeoncheongseok*, a kind of copper ore, for dark blue and navy blue colors and from malachite for dark greenish blue. These pigments were preferred because of their vividness, durability and relative serenity. In addition, the vermilion pigment produced from clay, also a popular color for *dancheong*, was mostly imported from China's western regions and was hence highly valued.

The painting of *dancheong* was done by *dancheongjangs*, artisans skilled in the work of *dancheong*. A *dancheongjang* artisan was referred to by a number of titles: *hwasa, hwagong, gachiljang,* or *dancheong*. When the artisan was also a monk, he was referred to as a *geumeo* or *hwaseung*.

For palace construction, *dancheong* was done by a governmental office, the *Seongonggam*. *Seongonggam* artisans exclusively carried out *dancheong* work for palaces and other places, such as guest houses and government buildings. Temples, on the other hand, had their own resident *dancheongjangs*. In addition to performing *dancheong* work , however, the temple artisans also engaged in production of other works, including Buddhist painting and sculpture. Although there were two different categories of *dancheongjang* for palace and temple painting , the technical procedures related to *dancheong* work were the same. The patterns and coloring systems were therefore identical for the two categories.

At the beginning of a project, a *pyeonsu*, or head artisan, was chosen by the initiating party of the construction project. The *pyeonsu* then selected the format of *dancheong* for the pertinent building and chose the patterns to be used. From

Dancheongjangs are artisans skilled in the work of *dancheong*. The tradition still lives on through a handful of superb *dancheongjangs*.

the mixing of colors to instruction about construction procedures, the *pyeonsu* was responsible for the completion of *dancheong* in its entirety.

Upon the beginning of *dancheong* work, a sample pattern was created for use in generating the same pattern of the pertinent parts of the building. This procedure was called *chulcho*. A bluish-green color was used as the base color, after which the pattern was placed on the desired spots of the building. This is done by pounding a powder sack over a paper transfer on which the design was outlined with pin holes. This work was referred to as *tacho*.

After the above procedures, coloring could finally be done. When coloring, each artisan painted only one color. The number of artisans employed in painting equalled the number of colors used in the design. Through such construction procedures, *dancheong* work was executed with efficiency.

Korea's *dancheong* developed in various different forms during 18th and 19th centuries. Shown here is *dancheong* on an old building.

Patterns

P atterns were devised by people to decorate their homes as well as articles for daily use including dress, furniture and various handicraft objects. Patterns are not only useful for ornamentation but symbolize human thought and philosophical and aesthetic pursuits.

Patterns often have their origins in early ideographs. They began as a means to express basic needs and feelings about one's surroundings and developed into a universal form of decorative art. Patterns can be largely divided into four main kinds based on motif-geometric patterns and patterns of plants, animals and other natural objects.

Geometric patterns in most cases consist of dots and lines forming symmetrical shapes. They include triangles, squares, diamonds, zigzags, latticeworks, frets, spirals, sawteeth, circles, ovals and concentric circles. It is interesting to note that most of these geometric patterns have their roots in primitive religious thought.

One example is the fret design. The lightning

One example of a highly-developed decorative art is the plant motifs on an old building.

pattern, which for primitive society depicted rain, represented their prayers for rainfall. A triangle symbolized reproduction and a woman's genitalia, and thus hope for childbirth. A swirl, resembling a whirlwind or a fern-brake, stood for death and the boundlessness of the universe.

Among favorite plant motifs were trees, flowers, fruits and grass. Animal designs engraved on stone or bone implements were related to the food-gathering activities of primitive humans such as hunting and fishing. Stone Age rock carvings feature various intriguing animal designs such as fish, whales, tigers, antlers and human figures. Natural objects include landscapes, rocks, waves and clouds. Next, ritual implements, weapons and personal

Geometric and animal patterns are two main motifs of Korean primitive art as shown in a rock carving in Goryeong.

Comb patterns can be found in articles made for daily use during the Neolithic Age. Shown here is earthenware decorated in a comb pattern (right).

ornaments from the Bronze Age show more diverse patterns executed with advanced technique.

Paleolithic sites on the Korean Peninsula maintain some traces of early patterns. It is believed, however, that patterns began to be used on everyday objects during the Neolithic Age. The comb patterns on the Neolithic earthenware are among the earliest examples. Abstract delineation grew increasingly popular with time, so that most of the Bronze Age mirrors were engraved with fine lines that formed triangles, circles, concentric circles, radiation and star shapes.

More naturalistic patterns were employed in the Three Kingdoms period (57 B.C.-A.D. 668) and motifs inspired by animism appeared in the Goguryeo King- 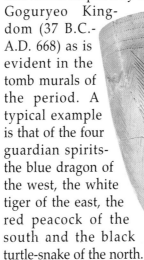 dom (37 B.C.- A.D. 668) as is evident in the tomb murals of the period. A typical example is that of the four guardian spirits- the blue dragon of the west, the white tiger of the east, the red peacock of the south and the black turtle-snake of the north.

Since ancient times, Koreans have used various patterns to decorate different objects. The ten longevity symbols shown decorate a wall from the late Joseon period.

Flower and other motifs on an old tile.

The *gwimyeon,* is one of the animal patterns found on a tile, Unified Silla era.

Abstract delineations in a mirror, Bronze Age.

These four Taoist symbols of auspiciousness and authority appear over and over in all forms of Korean art.

Linear renderings of symmetrically arranged quasiabstract phoenixes and dragons can be seen in many Silla (57 B.C.-A.D. 935) ornaments. But trees, antlers and bird wings, evidence of Siberian shamanistic traditions, are central to the motifs found in the crowns or pottery of Silla. The swirling cloud and flame motifs of Chinese origin decorate many personal ornaments and jewelry objects of Silla aristocrats. Honeysuckles and lotus flowers adorn the crowns of the Baekje Kingdom (18 B.C.-A.D. 660).

A combination of Buddhist designs with shamanistic, Taoist and Confucian motifs is found in the arts of all periods. Lotus flowers, clouds, lightning and swastikas can be seen in nearly every Buddhist structure or painting,

Flower-patterned latticeworks, with rhythmical and symmetrical shapes, give a very harmonious look. Latticeworks are frequently found in temples.

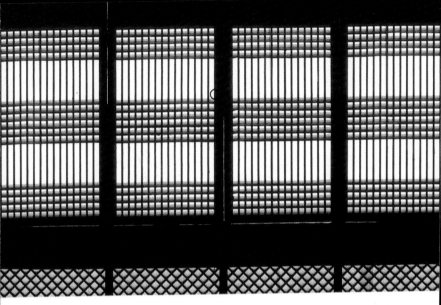

Wanja-patterned latticeworks imbue a sense of order.

either singly or in various configurations.

Following the unification of the peninsula by Silla, allied with Tang China in the seventh century, patterns grew more colorful and gorgeous with influences from China and Central Asia. Arabesques in the Tang style and Korean native style flower designs, called *bosanghwa*, were obviously of a more luxurious mode than the traditional honeysuckle and lotus patterns.

Delicate inlaid patterns on celadon, metalware and mother-of-pearl chests culminated the decorative art of the Goryeo period (918-1392), which was characterized by a flowering Buddhist culture. Inlaying was a technique of carving out a desired pattern on the surface of a piece of pottery or metal ware and filling in the recession with clay or gold or silver before coating the surface with glaze or lacquer. In

particular, Goryeo artists displayed adroit craftsmanship in bronzeware with silver inlay, which served as the foundation for the widely acclaimed inlaid celadon and mother-of-pearl articles in later years.

Naturalistic themes of leisurely, idealized life embellish many Goryeo celadonware and lacquered articles. Line drawings of water fowl, willows, reeds, chrysanthemums, cranes and clouds attest to the refined poetic taste of the Goryeo nobility. Other favorite motifs included the plum, orchid, and bamboo, which, together with the ubiquitous chrysanthemum, constituted the "four gentlemen" plants symbolizing the virtues of learned men of noble demeanor.

Many Goryeo celadon vases, incense burners and kundika bottles were skillfully adorned with drawings of water birds floating on willow-lined streams, carefree urchins frolicking among lotus leaves and wild geese flying against the clear autumn sky.

With the advent of the Joseon Dynasty (1392-1910), which adopted Confucianism as the basic creed for state administration and public ethics, the Buddhist-influenced, subtle and tasteful Goryeo-style decorative art gave way to relatively simpler styles reflecting the frugal lifestyle of a Confucian-dominated society. A preference for the simple and mono-chromatic is evident in the arts of this period.

The Joseon literati painting, characterized by simple but deft brushwork rendered in ink, finds a pleasant echo in the underglaze cobalt

This celadon *maebyeong*, or plum vase, with an inlaid cloud and crane design is a masterpiece of the Goryeo period. It exemplifies the exquisite and sophisticated technique developed during that period of inlaying patterns taken mostly from nature, such as birds, flowers or clouds.

The *taegeuk* is frequently seen in articles of daily use. Here the *taegeuk* pattern is found on a butterfly decorating a piece of furniture.

decoration of blue-and-white porcelain ware. Favorite motifs in both these genres included landscapes, flowers and birds, grapes, and the ever popular "four gentlemen" plants.

The coarse but charming *buncheong* ware deserves attention as a significant transitional stage connecting the elegant Goryeo celadon and the simple and pragmatic Joseon porcelain. Coated with white slip and glaze, the utilitarian stoneware vessels are ornamented with carefree peony scrolls, fish with humorous expressions and stamped tiny chrysan-themum heads, among other motifs frequently used.

Despite an obvious predilection for monochromic simplicity, the wooden bracketing systems, pillars and beams of palace and temple structures provide rare examples of dazzling decoration with patterns of all imaginable motifs

The *taegeuk* is the basic design motif of the Korean national flag. Shown here is the reprinted edition (left) and woodblock edition (right) used for printing the *taegeukgi* (Korean national flag).

rendered in the five cardinal colors of red, blue, yellow, white and black. Dragon and phoenix motifs adorn the ceilings of the throne halls of palaces symbolizing the king's supreme authority.

The ten longevity symbols constituted a major theme of folk painting as well as the decorative motifs of handicraft objects used by people of all social classes. The ten objects, including rocks, mountains, water, clouds, pine trees, turtles, deer, cranes, the fungus of immortality and the sun, made appealing motifs for folding screens, lacquered chests, ceramics and embroidery on clothes and other fabric items for daily use.

In the same Taoist strain of the world view, Chinese characters meaning longevity (*su*), happiness (*bok*), many sons (*danam*), and wealth and high social status (*bugwi*), were widely used in stylized or pictorial forms. These characters embellish various articles of everyday use such as pillow pads, spoon cases or wooden

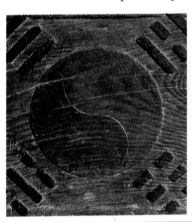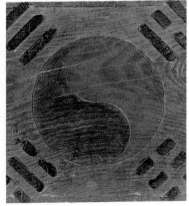

wardrobes.

Attesting to the deep-rooted, Taoist-Confucian tradition among the Koreans is the frequent use of the *taegeuk* pattern and the eight trigrams symbolizing possible situations and processes of the interaction between the two contrasting but mutually complementing elements of *eum*(Chin. yin) and *yang*.

The *taegeuk* pattern, consisting of two whirling elements, symbolizes the "Great Ultimate," or the primary source of all reality. The two whirls stand for *eum* and *yang*, the cosmic elements of tranquility and activity, weakness and strength, dark and light, and male and female.

Chu Hsi, the Chinese philosopher who founded Neo-Confucianism, said that the Great Ultimate is like the moon. It is one but its light is scattered upon rivers and lakes. Thus, he said, the Great Ultimate is both the sum total of all principles and principle in its oneness.

As seen in the Korean national flag, the pattern has *yang* in red at the top, and *eum* in blue at the bottom, symbolizing heaven and earth, respectively. Similar patterns of dualism are found on the doors of temples and shrines, clothes, furniture and daily objects such as fans or spoons.

Koreans march with *taegeukseon* fans in their hands during the 1988 Seoul Olympics, creating a beautiful wave of *taegeuk*.

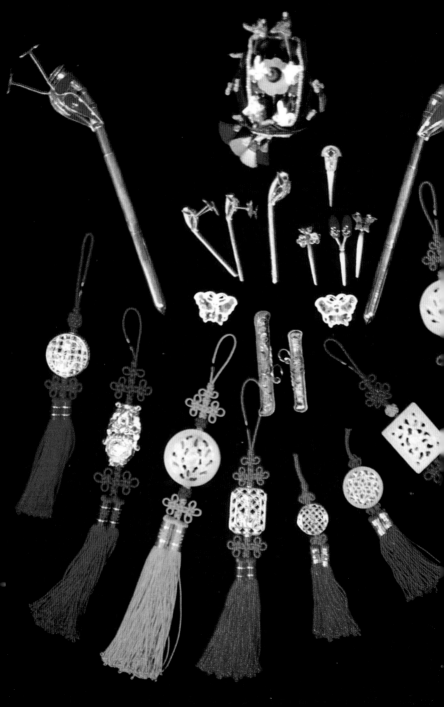

Jangsingu
Personal Ornaments

The term *Jangsingu* refers to various objects worn for ornamental purposes. In Korea, the original purpose of these ormaments was not only to enhance physical beauty but also to bring good luck and to drive out evil. The ornaments were also symbols reflecting the social status of the wearer. The history of these objects dates back to ancient times.

Tubular-shaped jade and necklaces made of animal bones were discovered among historical remains dating back to the Neolithic Age, and numerous relics from the Three Kingdoms period (57 B.C-A.D 668) include exquisitely detailed ornaments made of gold, silver and gilt bronze.

The most representative Korean ornaments include headdresses and hair accessories, necklaces, earrings, chest pieces, bracelets, court hats, ring, and pendants. Primitive hairpins and combs made of animal bones are some of the hair ornaments that date from prehistoric times.

Hair ornaments from the third and fourth centuries were more delicate and splendid, and include combs, rod hairpins, and clasps used to

The history of personal ornaments in Korea dates back to ancient times. Shown are various traditional ornaments worn by women.

hold hair together. Combs discovered inside the ancient tombs of the Silla Kingdom (57 B.C.-A.D. 935) were all made of lacquered wood, and the teeth were fairly thin and long. A hair clasp discovered inside the tombs of King Muryeong(r. 501-523) of Baekje resembles an elegant bird in flight with a head part followed by three long branches detailed to look like the billowing tails of a bird. Hairpins from the Goryeo Dynasty (918-1392) are even more delicate and exquisite in their details, with a Chinese phoenix or rooster heads carved on the head parts.

Golden necklace, Silla Kingdom.

Another object from the Goryeo Dynasty is the topknot hairpin, which was used by men to hold their topknots in place. In addition to this practical purposes, it also served as an ornamental piece. Magnificent gold topknot hairpins from the Goryeo Dynasty came in various shapes and sizes.

During the Joseon Dynasty (1392-1910) a national policy was declared imposing limits on the use of personal ornaments. Tight restraints on the use of gold and silver brought about a

An ornamental comb decorated with golden flowers, Unified Silla period.

deterioration in the artistic value of the ornaments produced during this period and in the quality of craftsmanship in general. However, as a result, the production of ornaments using materials other than gold and silver flourished, and their use became widely popularized .

During the Joseon Dynasty, the use of rod hairpins was severely restricted, with social status dictating the use of different materials and shapes. Women of the royal court and high society wore rod pins made of gold, silver, pearls, jade, and coral, while those of lesser status were limited to ones made of wood, horn, nickel alloy, and brass.

The head shapes of the rod pins were also different according to social status. The queen and women of the royal court and high society wore pins shaped in the images of dragons and Chinese phoenixes, while common folk were allowed only plain pins or those shaped like

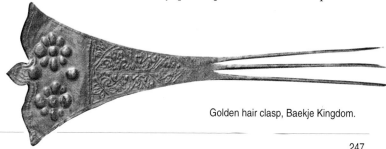

Golden hair clasp, Baekje Kingdom.

mushrooms. The head shapes and materials of the pins also varied according to the season.

Several new shapes of ceremonial hair decorations including the *cheopji* and *tteoljam*, as well as hair picks and *daenggi* (ribbons) emerged during the Joseon Dynasty. The *cheopji*, is a type of hairpin that women wore with ceremonial dress to enhance their beauty. It came in the shape of a phoenix or a frog. The phoenix-shaped pin was reserved for the queen's exclusive use, and the frog-shaped pin was for common folk. *Tteoljam* was worn by women of high society on ceremonial occasions. It came in round, square, and butterfly shapes and a variety of other forms. The pieces were lavishly decorated with cloisonné, pearls, and other precious gems.

Hair picks refer to all the ornamental pieces worn in chignons other than the rod pins. These include plain picks with pointed ends and practical ones that could be used as ear picks and also for parting one's hair. Chrysanthemums, lotus, apricot blossoms, and butterflies were some of the more popular shapes, and the picks were decorated with coral, jade, precious stones, cloisonné, and pearls. A *daenggi* (hair ribbon) was a piece of gold-inlaid cloth that was used to hold a woman's hair in a braid. The ribbons came in a variety of shapes and sizes.

Along with these hair decorations, Koreans

Magnificent topknot hairpins in various shapes and sizes (right).

Cheopjis shaped like a phoenix (above) and a frog (below) worn by women in the royal court during the Joseon Dynasty (right).

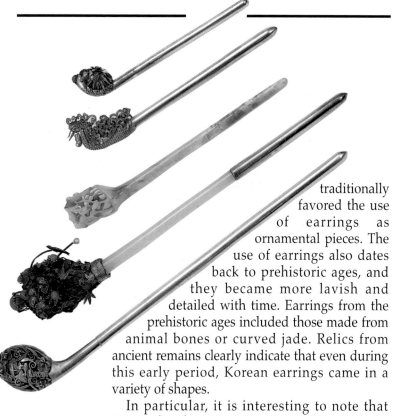

traditionally favored the use of earrings as ornamental pieces. The use of earrings also dates back to prehistoric ages, and they became more lavish and detailed with time. Earrings from the prehistoric ages included those made from animal bones or curved jade. Relics from ancient remains clearly indicate that even during this early period, Korean earrings came in a variety of shapes.

In particular, it is interesting to note that during the Three Kingdoms period (57 B.C.-A.D 668), earrings were popualr with both men and women. Earrings from that period can be divided into three groups according to their shapes: a single loop, a

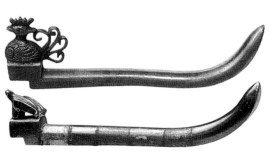

loop attached to the post, and those with multiple loops with lavish decorations dangling from one of them.

Tteoljam lavishly decorated with cloisonné, pearls, and other precious gems, Joseon Dynasty.

Materials used for earrings included gold, silver, and gilt bronze, with gold being the most popular. Among the relics of the Goryeo Dynasty are pure gold earrings. Some are simple in design with three connected loops, while others are decorated with round beads. While the use of earrings wasn't as popular during the Joseon Dynasty, the period is noteworthy in that it brought about a revolutinary change in the way earrings were worn. Until then, earrings were worn by piercing a person's earlobes and inserting the posts but it was now possible to simply clasp them on the helices. Sometimes five-colored tassels were used to complement the simple ornamentation of the earrings. These types of earrings were reserved for ceremonial purposes and were not for everyday use.

Hair picks worn in chignons, Joseon Dynasty.

The use of necklaces in Korea dates back to prehistoric times. During that period they were constructed from a variety of materials including animal teeth, bones, tubular jade, and jade stones. From the third to the seventh centuries, the use of necklaces grew more popular. The shapes became more diverse as well, and necklaces were worn as a single strand or in multiple (two, three, four, or six) strands. The more popular materials were gold and jade.

Chest ornaments are objects worn on the chest for decorative purposes and differ from necklaces according to their lengths. During prehistoric times, primitive chest ornaments were made by drilling holes into sea shells and connecting them with a piece of string.

Chest ornaments of the Silla Kingdom became much more lavish and exquisite in detail. In particular, the chest ornament discovered inside the *Geumnyeongchong* (Tomb of the Golden Bell) is spectacular in its beauty and is lavishly decorated

A *daenggi* was a piece of gold-impressed cloth used to hold a woman's hair in a braid, Joseon Dynasty (left).
Gold decorated earring, Silla Kingdom (right).

with 152 glass beads. Another piece found inside *Hwangnamdaechong* (The Great tomb at Hwangnam) is also exquisitely decorated with gold, silver, glass and jade.

One article of ornamentation that was widely popular throughout the history of Korea is the bracelet, whose use dates back to ancient times. Early bracelets were primitive, made from sea shells, but with time the use of a variety of materials such as bronze, jade, and glass became more widespread. Bracelets, along with earrings and rings were the most popular ornaments during the Three Kingdoms period. The discovery of numerous bracelets in relics from this period attests to this fact, and most of these were made from jade, glass and metal.

The finger ring was another popular piece of ornamentation throughout the history of Korea. As early as in prehistoric times, Koreans are known to have used rings for decorative purposes. A ring made from a piece of bronze plate was dug up from an ancient tomb dating back to prehistoric times, which testifies to its early use.

From the Silla Kingdom, numerous silver

rings have been discovered, and the lavish and exquisite details on these pieces clearly attest to the high quality of crafts-manship of this period.

Necklace (above); gold and silver bracelet(below), Silla Kingdom.

Representative rings of the Goryeo Dynasty are a gold ring decorated with agate and another with green gemstones. Others include a pure gold ring with an embossed arabesque pattern, a silver ring with jagged design, a silver ring with exquisite engravings, and a plain copper ring without any ornamental design.

During the Joseon Dynasty, rings were the most popular ornaments along with pendants. The materials used to make these rings were also diverse; they include gold, silver, cloisonné, jade, agate, amber, green jade, pearl, and bronze.

Court hats and crowns were worn by the king and government officials. In addition to their ornamental purposes, they served to represent the wearer's social status. The higher a person's position, the more lavish the hat. During the Three Kingdoms (Goguryeo, Baekje and Silla) period, each kingdom with its

Milhwa ring, Joseon Dynasty.

different social structure developed its unique style of court hat. Among those of Goguryeo, the most outstanding is the gold court hat created in the image of a burning flame. This gold hat was constructed by attaching nine ornaments, each shaped to resemble a burning flame, on a gilt bronze plate. Two identical ornaments were then attached to either side of the hat for additional decoration. A gold court hat excavated in Hwaseong-ri in Daedong-gun boasts a frontal ornamental piece resembling a half-moon.

A gold court crown discovered in an ancient tomb in the Bannam area of Naju dates back to the Baekje Kingdom. This crown is decorated with lavish ornaments on the broad front band and on each side. The most impressive crowns of Baekje are the ones discovered among the relics inside the tomb of King Muryeong. The decorations on these crowns, presumed to have been worn by the king and queen, were cut from thin gold plates and created in the images of glowing haloes.

Among the most widely known crowns of Silla is the one with five ornaments attached to a narrow band. Additional decorations on the

Gold court hats, Silla Kingdom (above right) and Baekje (below right).

three main ornaments on the front and on each of the sides resemble tiny twigs branching out of a tree, thereby creating cascading images of small mountains. During the Goryeo Dynasty, crown styles were deeply influenced by the Chinese: *Myeollyugwan* was a square, flat crown with dangling strings of small precious stones that was worn by the king with formal attire; *Wonyugwan* was a dark, silk hat with a jade ornament worn by the king when meeting his court; *Bokdu* was a formal hat worn by those who had passed the highest civil service examination when receiving their appointments; and, *Samo* was a round, black silk hat worn by civil and military officials, and is donned these days by the groom in a traditional wedding ceremony. Court hats similar to those worn by the Chinese were still popular during the Joseon Dynasty. It was not until

mid-Joseon that the *gat*, a uniquely Korean hat woven from horse-hair, emerged. Jade buttons and decorative egret shapes and strings were attached to the *gat* for ornamental purposes. Women's hats also grew more lavish as jewels were attached to flower hats and bridal tiaras, rendering them more appropriate for special ceremonies.

The most representative item of personal ornamentation from the Joseon Dynasty is the pendant. Pendants, worn by women on the outer bows or inner bows of their blouses or on their skirts, were very popular during this period. Materials included metals such as gold, silver and bronze and gemstones such as white jade, green jade, agate, red jade, blue stones, pure jade, rough diamond, and malachite. The use of precious stones and shells including amber, coral, pearl, and tortoise shell was also common. The pendants also came in a variety of designs with some resembling animals such as bats, turtles, butterflies, ducks, goldfish, cicadas, and terrapins while others were shaped like plants including peppers, eggplants, clusters of grapes, acorns, and walnuts. Often the shapes were taken from objects that were part of everyday life,

Personal ornaments, Joseon Dynasty flower crown (left) and pendant (right).

and some pendants resemble bottles, pouches, bells, gourds, drums, hourglass drums, and spectacle cases.

Another personal item women carried was the ornamental dagger. These were used for decorative purposes as well as for self-defense. The cylindrical dagger and others shaped like the letter "Z", squares, and octagons are only a few of the variety of shapes representative of this period.

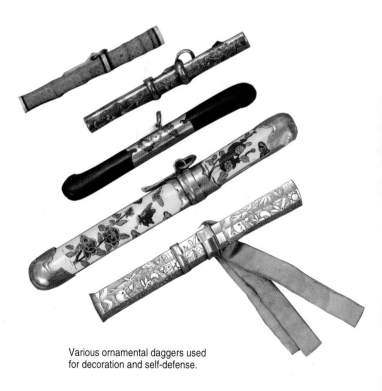

Various ornamental daggers used for decoration and self-defense.

Jasu
Embroidery

Jasu, or embroidery, appears to have begun from the prehistoric era when the human race first started to make clothes. People used needles made out of bones of fish or animals to sew and weave animal skins and the bark or leaves of trees. Later, as civilization gradually developed, clothes began to be made, and with the advent of metal needles, embroidery emerged.

From then on, *jasu* developed as an art used to decorate textiles, and it, like the embroidery of other cultures, reflects that the nation's particular living environment, customs, and religion.

Korean *jasu* has a long history. As times changed, it expressed the Koreans ideal of beauty. Along with weaving and sewing, *jasu* was a method of cultivating beauty in every corner of daily life. Sincere efforts went into every stitch and required delicate dexterity. The full expression of Korean character can be found in *jasu*.

Among the Korean prehistoric excavated relics, a *bangchucha* (a spindle cart) that was

Korean embroidery fully expresses the Korean character. Embroided *Sipjangsaeng*, the 10 longevity symbols.

made out of earth or stone, big and small bone needles and stone needles, and needle pouches were found. Based on the finding of such weaving tools, it is clear that weaving and sewing existed during that period. Throughout the Bronze and Iron Ages, metal equipment for farming developed, thereby remarkably improving the farming industry.

In Korea, *ma* (hemp) and *ppong* (mulberry) trees were cultivated; *myeonpo* (cotton cloth) and *mapo* (hemp cloth), as well as *hapsa* (twisted thread), were also produced. The development of weaving became the fundamental prerequisite for the development of *jasu*, and *jasu* was used to represent the status and rank of the ruling class in the form of decoraton on clothes, flags, or, wagons.

During the Three Kingdoms period, overall production technology developed greatly. Accordingly, weaving machines were improved and textile skills advanced; not only a variety of textile was produced, but also the quality improved. Naturally *jasu* became popular. A trace of *jasu* that was embroidered with golden thread was found among the relics in the *Cheonmachong* (Tomb of the Heavenly Horse) in Gyeongju, a good example that shows the status of *jasu* culture during that period.

During the Unified Silla period, horse saddles and things related to everyday life, not to mention clothes, were decorated with *jasu*. Buddhist *jasu* was also commonly created.

Particularly during the 9th year (834) of King Heungdeok, a prohibition on clothing style was pronounced to strictly regulate the usage of textiles according to the *golpum* (aristocratic rank) system. During this period, due to the prosperity of Buddhism, much of the nobility eagerly gave donations for the construction or decoration of temples. As such a phenomenon accelerated, King Aejang prohibited construction of new temples and allowed only the repair of existing temples to be done to prevent the waste of materials. Usage of golden threads in Buddhist items was also prohibited. This indicates that high quality silk and *jasu* was used even in decorating objects in the *beopdang*, the main halls of Buddhist temples.

Gongbangs (artisan shops) existed that were in charge of weaving, dyeing, and sewing. Artisans exported silk to China, and dyeing techniques were greatly improved at this time. Developments in dyeing techniques became a

The cultivation of hemp (left top) and mulberry (left bottom), and the subsequent development of weaving were prerequisite to the development of Korean embroidery.

major factor that enabled the diversification and delicate coloring of textiles and threads.

In the Goryeo Dynasty, *jasu* became excessively luxurious. *Jasu* of that era, for convenience sake, can be classified into *boksik jasu*, *giyong jasu*, *gamsang jasu*, and Buddhist *jasu*.

Boksik jasu refers to *jasu* embroidered to decorate clothing. Dress was strictly regulated according to status and rank. For example, during the 3rd year (1034) of the reign of King Deokjong, children and women were prohibited from wearing golden ornamental hairpins or embroidered silk clothes. During the 9th year (1043) of Jeongjong's reign, ordinary men and women were prohibited from decorating silk with dragon–or phoenix–patterns, along with golden stitches.

Also, during the 22nd year (1144) of King Injong's reign (1144), the King prohibited the use of golden thread in clothing and jade decoration in bowls. It can be inferred that during that era *boksik jasu* was more than simply delicate and refined; it became excessively luxurious.

The queen and noble women of that time enjoyed red clothing with *jasu* decorations. The guardsmen who escorted the king largely wore silk clothes with flowers in five colors or bird patterns, and their belts were also often decorated with embroidered flowers in five colors.

Giyong jasu embroidery decorated various materials used in the king's palace.

Gamsang jasu was embroidery which

The tradition of Goryeo (918-1392) *giyong jasu*, or the embroidery for the royal palace, is reflected in this folding screen decorated with the private seals of past kings.

developed as a type of artistic work. In other words, by use of *jasu*, various ornamental materials were decorated. Such *jasu* was prevalently used in folding screens in the bedroom or living room.

Buddhist *jasu* was embroidery related to Buddhism. During the Goryeo Dynasty, Buddhism, as a means of defending the nation and promoting prosperities, was supported as the national religion. As a result, more than in any other era, Buddhism became very prosperous, and *jasu* was heavily used in the statues of Buddha or various temples.

During the Joseon Dynasty, marked changes occurred in many aspects of the country: political, economical, social, and cultural. Due to its early advocacy of an agriculture-first policy as its basic principle and the suppression of commercial industry, the handicraft industry did not develop. As a result, farmers concentrated on the production of food as their main occupation, and manual handicrafts became a secondary business. In spite of such circumstances, the production of clothing was prominent.

Accordingly, the textile industry related to production of clothing, as well as weaving and dyeing, generally became the responsibility of women. Female workers were encouraged to perform such work to increase productivity. It was also emphasized as a prerequisite virtue for every woman.

The legislation of the *hyungbae* (official insignia) system in the early Joseon Dynasty was indeed note-worthy. Such a system, which was related to the development of *jasu*, required the systemization of government offices' manual work. The organization of the *gwancheong* (governmental offices) manual work increased from the Three Kingdoms era through the Goryeo Dynasty. It peaked during the 15th century, which was the early part of the Joseon

A study of *hyungbae*, the embroidered emblems of official rank, is helpful in understanding the development of embroidery during the Joseon Dynasty (1392-1910).

Hyungbae of cranes and tigers.

Dynasty.

Hyungbae refers to the embroidered emblems that represented the rank of the government's civil and military officials. It was first implemented during the first year (1453) of King Danjong's reign. Later, after several modifications, the *hyungbae* system was improved and the emblems gradually became luxurious.

As a type of a publicly-used embroidery, *hyungbae jasu* is good reference material in understanding the development of embroidery of that period. Artisans who were mobilized to produce textiles, and related items such as *hyungbae,* were among the most skilled people in the nation; they were placed in the central and regional governmental offices and devoted themselves to this field. They were responsible for the production of clothing and other textile products and embroidery decorations that were used by the royal family and high-ranking governmental officials.

Besides these organizations, there was an additional organization called the *subang* (embroidery room) that was exclusively responsible for the embroidery of clothes and miscellaneous materials for the family of the

The embroidery on the king's state ceremonial dress symbolizes his high social status and authority.

king. Upon completion of a certain level of education and expertise, women were selected to enter the palace to work in the *subang* and were registered; they exclusively produced *jasu* to meet the demands of the palace. During the Joseon Dynasty, interrelations among various artisan organizations and the *subang* provided the cornerstone of the palace *jasu*, which is also called *gungsu*. The *gungsu* tradition was sustained until the end of the Joseon Dynasty, and due to the standard format and the advanced skills of the artisans, the embroidery was delicate and perfectly executed.

In contrast with *gungsu*, there was *minsu* (folk embroidery) that was produced by the common people. Unlike *gungsu* that was specialized, *minsu* was a domestic skill passed down through the family or the region, and women in the household were in charge. As a result, in comparison with *gungsu* that was standardized, *minsu* reflected the characteristics of the individuals who created it. If Korean traditional *jasu* is classified according to function, it can be divided into *byeongpung* (folding screen) *jasu*, *boksik jasu* (decorating clothes and accessories used in the home), and Buddhist *jasu*.

Embroidered folding screens played an important role in major events in life. For example, they were widely used at congratulatory banquets, such as those for anniversaries, birthdays especially the 60th birthday and engagements and for mourning ceremonies and other rites.

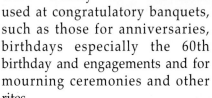

Embroidered folding screens were not only used in the various rooms of the home, but also in temples and shrines, as well as in the palaces, guest houses and lecture rooms.

The *byeongpung jasu*, therefore, exhibited great variety. The majority of screens, however, were of flowers and birds, the *sipjangsaeng*, or 10 longevity symbols, and subok, or Chinese characters for "long life" and "happiness." For flower and bird screens, the peony, chrysanthemum, water lily, plum tree, and paulownia trees were matched with a couple of pheasants, a mandarin duck, phoenixes or ducks to symbolize a happy family. The *sipjangsaeng* are ten natural objects symbolizing long life: the sun, clouds, mountains, water, pine, bamboo, crane, deer, turtles and the fungus of immortality.

There were many other embroidery designs, usually pertaining to lucky omens and

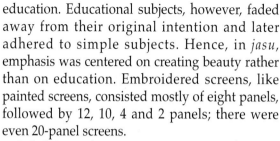

Hwarot, the ceremonial dress for the women of the palace, were luxuriously decorated with embroidered flowers and symbols of luck and longevity.

The queen's emblem was decorated with a dragon or phoenix.

education. Educational subjects, however, faded away from their original intention and later adhered to simple subjects. Hence, in *jasu*, emphasis was centered on creating beauty rather than on education. Embroidered screens, like painted screens, consisted mostly of eight panels, followed by 12, 10, 4 and 2 panels; there were even 20-panel screens.

Boksik jasu refers to embroidery on clothes and accessories. Particularly during the Joseon Dynasty, dress styles were highly differentiated according to class and rank, and patterns used in *jasu* followed such distinctions. To represent high social status and authority, dresses worn in the palace usually had golden stitches or colored threads. *Jasu* was done in two styles: one was embroidering on the surface of the clothes directly, another was attaching *jasu* applique to the clothes. The first was used for the king's state ceremonial dress and various ceremonial dresses for the king's family members; the latter included miscellaneous dress embroidery, such as the embroidered patches on the breast and on the back of official uniforms.

On a *hwarot*, which was the ceremonial dress for the women in the palace, patterns of various flowers, such as peonies, chrysanthemums, fungus of immortality, and herbs, as well as various lucky omens and patterns of longevity were luxuriously embroidered. The clothing of males in the royal family and government officials did not have embroidery directy on the surface of the cloth; instead *hyungbae* decorated

1

2

3

4

5

in patterns of cranes or tigers were attached to everyday clothing. *Pyojang*, an emblem which was attached to the dress of the king and queen, on the other hand, was differentiated from *hyungbae* and called *bo;* its embroidery consisted of dragons or phoenixes.

For the most part, common people were not allowed to wear embroidered clothes, except for a *hwarot*, or ceremonial dress, at the time of their wedding. Other materials that were embroidered included children's hats, vests, and belts. Especially, embroidered clothing for children used various colors and matching patterns to express their innocence.

Jasu also decorated numerous items used in the home. It would be impossible to list them all, but they include pillow cases, eyeglass cases, cushions and pouches for such thing as tobacco, spoons and chopsticks and brushes.

Unlike embroidery for purely decorative purposes, Buddhist *jasu*, which decorated temples and Buddhist statues, was created out of religious devotion. They were executed with extreme care by artisans of extraordinary expertise. Accordingly, there are many masterpieces which are preserved in temples and museums.

Everyday items:
1. Pillow case
2. Pouch
3. Pouch for spoon and chopsticks
4. Belt for *ham* (a bridal gift chest)
5. Belt and pouch for a 1-year old baby

Paper Crafts

Koreans have a centuries-old history of paper-making and have long enjoyed using indigenous good-quality paper.

Korea's oldest paper, called *maji*, was made from hemp. *Maji* is produced using roughly the following process:

Scraps of hemp or ramie cloth are soaked in water for some time and then shredded into tiny pieces. These pieces are ground in a grindstone to produce a slimy pulp, which then is steamed, cleansed with water, ground and placed in a tank. This raw material is pressed onto a frame and sun-dried while being bleached. This method of papermaking was most popular during the Three Kingdoms period (57 B.C.-A.D. 668).

In Baekje (18 B.C.-A.D. 660), one of the Three Kingdoms, paper thus made served as a chief medium for documenting historical events in the second half of the fourth century. Notably, Damjing, a Korean Buddhist monk and painter

Korea's traditional paper craft lives on.

of Goguryeo (37 B.C-A.D. 668), another of the Three Kingdoms, introduced techniques of papermaking to Japan in 610, the 21st year of Goguryeo's King Yeongyang. From all this, it is obvious that Korea had already developed an advanced method of papermaking by the early part of the seventh century.

In the Goryeo era (918-1392), Koreans began to make paper from mulberry bark, or *dangnamu*, which made it possible to produce paper in large quantities, and in the 11th century, Korea began exporting paper to China. Between the 23rd year (1145) of King Injong and the 18th year (1188) of King Myeongjong, mulberries were grown virtually all over the Korean Peninsula as the private paper manufacturing industry became a thriving business. The Government encouraged papermaking by setting up a *jiso*, an administrative agency designed exclusively to promote the production of mulberry paper. Eventually, Goryeo succeeded in producing fairly thick and sturdy paper whose obverse and reverse sides are both quite smooth and glossy. In later years, Korea's papermaking techniques further advanced, leading to the production of

A paper sewing box.

hanji, a traditional Korean paper.

Along with the indigenous and ingenious development of papermaking, Korea has established a deep-rooted tradition in the versatile use of paper. Among numerous traditional items of papercraft were such household goods as wardrobes, cabinets, chests, boxes, calligraphy desks, writing-brush holders, candlestands, room curtains, mats, cushions, comb holders and comb cabinets, trays, bowls with lids, basins, jars and food coverings. Other popular papercrafts included tobacco pouches, spectacle cases, dippers, quivers, soldiers' armor, fans, umbrellas, apparel, footwear and hats, as

well as artificial flowers, lanterns, and kites.

It is hard to tell exactly when Koreans began to produce this plethora of items from paper, many of them for household use. However, historical documents indicate that the popular use of paper items dates as far back as the Three Kingdoms (57 B.C.-A.D. 668). This period left many books documenting important historical and other data. During that period, Korea

introduced the method of papermaking to Japan and exported much-acclaimed Korean paper to China.

Interestingly, the great compilation known as the *Samgungnyusa* (Memorabilia of the Three Kingdoms) notes that Koreans enjoyed making and flying kites made of paper, a clear indication that papercraft had already been developed to a considerable extent in Korea by that time.

In the early period of Joseon, under the reign of King Taejo, a decree was proclaimed to emphasize austerity. Accordingly, artificial flowers made of paper replaced virtually all floral decorations at the sites of royal and private banquets and other functions from the beginning of the Joseon era. Artificial flowers most commonly used during the pre-Joseon period of Goryeo were made of wax or silk cloth. During the reign of King Sejong (r.1418-1450), the use of paper flowers, in lieu of other kinds of artificial flowers, was further extended to Buddhist rites and festivals.

Paper flowers and paper lanterns first used in Buddhist rites and festivals during the reign of King Sejong are still used today.

As the demand for paper increased rapidly, the royal court of King Sejong established a special office in charge of papermaking, leading to mass production of paper. During the early period of Joseon, the royal court supplied troops guarding the remote northern frontiers with *jigap*, armor made of specially treated paper. This armor was not only waterproof, but also effectively protected the soldiers from the severe cold during winter. More importantly, this armor was sturdy enough to serve as a protective covering against arrows, spears, swords, or other weapons. During the period of King Injo, *jigap* was steadily improved, often using scraps of paper and waste paper as raw materials. *Jigap* also inspired the invention of civilian attire made of treated paper.

As time passed, paper gained increasingly wider usage. For example, fans made of silk, widely used by Korean nobles, gave way to fans made of paper. In the middle period of Joseon, when tobacco began to be imported, tobacco pouches made of paper appeared and became the vogue. Other paper products made of old books and other used paper also made their debut.

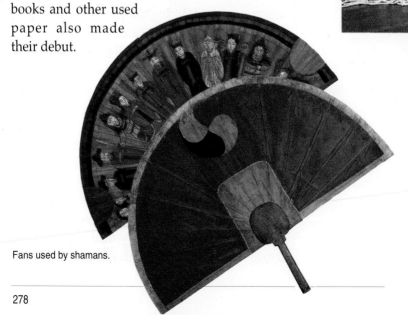

Fans used by shamans.

A Human Cultural Treasure makes various household goods by weaving paper cords.

Frugality was considered a virtue in daily life. True to the spirit, Koreans came up with many other ways to make good use of scraps of paper. Paper reproduced from scraps of paper was used as lining for the walls of rooms. Scraps of paper were made into string that was durable enough to be used as a ring (in lieu of a door knob) attached to a door or as a clothesline.

In the early 18th century, Koreans began to produce cushions and mats made by weaving paper cords dyed in various colors. Subsequently, a variety of other household and personal items made of paper cords emerged.

According to Korean folklore, if one collects hair that falls out while combing one's hair and burns it outside the front door of one's home in the twilight of Lunar New Year's Day, it will ward off diseases and other evils. This folk custom made popular a bag made of oiled paper for keeping this hair. Also popular for the same reason was a comb cabinet.

In most cases, paper made from mulberry bark was used for traditional paper crafts. More specifically, second-hand mulberry paper – calligraphy-practice sheets, scraps left over from bookmaking or papering walls or the pages of old books—was especially favored. Traditional paper that was dyed various colors and oiled

A Korean mask, *Tal*, made with the *jido gibeop* technique.

1. Chest, placed at the head of the bedding.
2. Shoe made of paper cord.
3. Oil lamp stand.
4. Comb holder.
5. Tray.

was also used.

Korea's traditional papercrafts can be divided into three major categories depending on the way the paper is used and on the shape of the items created. These categories are *jido gibeop*, *jiho gibeop* and *jiseung gibeop*.

In *jido gibeop*, many sheets of paper are pasted together and then this multilayered, sturdy paper is shaped into a desired form. The products thus made ranged from tobacco pouches and workbaskets to needle cases and comb cabinets. Also in this category are paper products made by pasting many layers of paper on both the outside and inside of a pre-shaped bamboo or wooden frame. Products made through this technique included wardrobes and trunks.

Colored paper was used mainly for such products as wardrobes and trunks used by women. Favorite colors were blue, red, yellow, green and purple, all obtained from natural dyestuffs manufactured at home. Often, colored paper was cut into the shape of a butterfly, a bat, a mandarin duck, the double-letter Chinese character meaning happiness, or the Buddhist reverse swastika and pasted onto paper products to wish for good luck.

Jiho gibeop is the technique of using "paper clay" to make such kitchen items as bowls with lids and large scooped bowls. Paper clay is made

A jewelry box (left).
A letter holder (right).

from scraps of paper that are soaked in water and then crushed and mixed with an ample dose of glue.

Jiseung gibeop applies to the technique of making paper cords and weaving them into a broad range of household goods such as baskets, mesh bags, jars and trays. Other popular items made by weaving paper cords included stationery cases, mats, cushions and curtains. Still other paper cord products included quivers, dippers, powder-flasks, footwear, washbasins and chamber pots.

Some paper cord products including small calligraphy desks and trays were reinforced with wooden bars to withstand the weight of the goods placed on them. *Jiseung gibeop* developed during the Joseon period, is a unique technique that enabled craftsmen to put otherwise useless scraps of paper to good use.

Most of these Korean paper products were properly varnished to enhance their appearance and durability while making them waterproof, since the use of lacquer for varnishing was rather discouraged under government regulations, the most commonly used varnish was *sichil*, a mixture of unripened persimmon juice, rice glue and perilla oil. Colored papercrafts were often covered by liquified agar-agar and *beobyeonyu*, a mixture of litharge, talc and alum which were boiled down in perilla oil.

All in all, Korean papercraft has long established itself as an ingenious part of the nation's creative and versatile folk culture.

Long-time papercraft collector shows various papercraft items.

Bojagi
Wrapping Cloths

T he word *bojagi* or *bo* for short, refers to square hemmed cloths of various size, color, and design, which Koreans used to wrap, store, or carry things. *Bojagi* was not only practical and versatile items in the daily lives of Koreans, but also very artistic. *Bo* attests to the artfulness that Koreans seek even in the most mundane aspects of their everyday lives.

The use of *bojagi* in Korea dates back to time immemorial, and historical records show the many ways in which they have been used. Although *bojagi* was created for everyday use, they also added flair and style to various ceremonies and rituals. During the Joseon Dynasty, the patterns and designs became particularly colorful. Because they are so easily folded and take up such little space, they could easily fit into, and become a colorful part of,

Bojagi was not only practical, but also very artistic.
Jogakbo with triangular shapes.

everyday Korean customs and practices.

Bojagi's place in Korean culture began in part with the folk religions of ancient times, when it was believed that keeping something wrapped was tantamount to keeping good fortune. A typical illustration would be the use of *bojagi* to wrap wedding gifts. Elaborate needlework is applied to such wrapping to wish the bride and groom much luck in their new life together.

Patchwork *bojagi* particularly reflects Korean artistic flair. *Bojagi* was born out of the habit of Korean housewives to make good use of small, otherwise useless pieces of leftover cloth by patching them up into useful wrappers. As time went by, the patchwork itself became a highly creative and artistic craft.

Embroidery of various figures and characters also adds to the beauty of *bojagi*. The handicraft can often reach the beauty of levels of artistic accomplishment. Embroidered *bojagi* is known as *subo*, the prefix *su* meaning "embroidery."

A popular motif on *subo* is trees, which to Koreans have represented the most sacred of living things. Since ancient times, Koreans have worshipped trees as the physical embodiment of sacred spirits and miracles. The trees on *subo*, therefore, bespeak of the prayers of their creators for good fortune.

Other favorite motifs for *subo*, include flowers, fruits, mandarin ducks and other symbols of goodness, which reflected the Korean well-wishing that goes into the making of *bojagi*. Each symbol represented something; for example,

Bojagi embodies the Korean artistic flair. *Jogakbo* with triangular shape (above), traditional *bojagi* with flower motif (middle), and rainbow-striped *bo* (below).

pomegranate stood for many births and many sons. The basic colors of *subo* are blue, red, yellow, white, and black, the fundamental colors of nature as postulated in the *eum-yang*, theory of five primary elements (metal, wood, water, fire, and earth), an important element in the way Koreans understood the workings of the universe. *Bojagi* have thus been closely related to the everyday beliefs and practices of Koreans. They are convenient and safe carriers and protectors. As such, they perform the same functions as the western bags, but are far more versatile. Bags and luggage generally have standard sizes, but there was no standard size for *bojagi*. It would be difficult to find a western bags that can fit a watermelon without the loss of much space; however, a *bojagi* will do the job splendidly.

Koreans have farming origins, and in the quiet, peaceful existence of their agricultural communities, they have always had a tendency to find playfulness and beauty in the most mundane things in life. The colorful

Jogakbo is notable for its elegant design. *Mosi jogakbo* (above) and *jogakbo* made with colorful patches of cloth (below).

Koreans still use *bojagi* made with leftover cloth.

bojagi culture is one result of their inclination to combine the practical and the pleasing. As the centuries went by, the craftsmanship became even more elaborate and diverse, and *bojagi* came to embody the artistic sensibilities of everyday Koreans.

The many uses of *bojagi* can be categorized as follows:

1. *Sangyongbo* (daily use *bo*):
   Jeondaebo (money belt *bo*) to wrap things (such as money) in and tie around the waste or shoulder;
   Bobusangbo (backpack merchant *bo*) used by petty merchants to carry their goods;
   Sangbo (table *bo*) to cover table with;
   Ibulbo (blanket *bo*) to wrap blanket in;
   Ppallaebo (laundry *bo*) to wrap laundry items in;

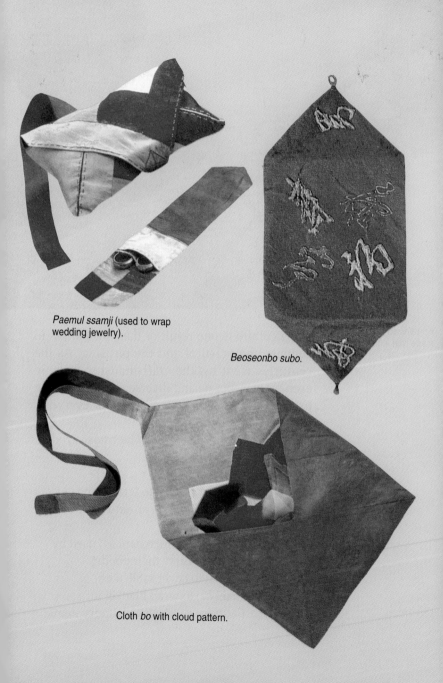

Paemul ssamji (used to wrap wedding jewelry).

Beoseonbo subo.

Cloth *bo* with cloud pattern.

A popular motif on *subo* are trees. *Yeonhwamun ham batchimbo* (a gift chest was placed here).

Subo with flower motif.

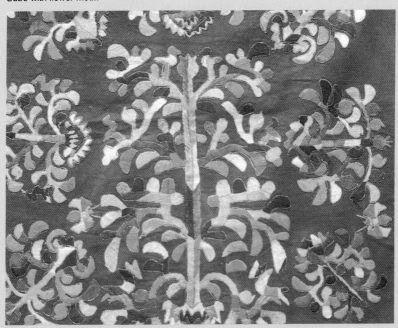

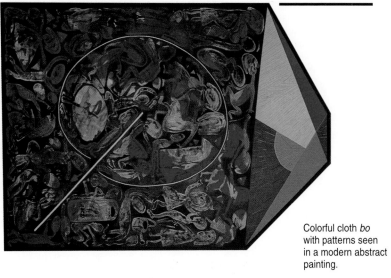

Colorful cloth *bo* with patterns seen in a modern abstract painting.

Beoseonbo (socks *bo*) to keep socks in;
Chaekbo (book *bo*) to keep and carry books in;
Hwaettaebo (hanger *bo*) to cover clothes racks with;
Ganchalbo (letter *bo*) to keep letters and documents in;
Gyeongdaebo (dresser *bo*) to cover a dressing stand with.

2. *Hollyeyongbo* (wedding *bo*):
   Hambo (gift chest *bo*) to wrap the ham in;
   Gireogibo (wild geese *bo*) to wrap the ceremonial pair of wild geese in;
   Yedanbo (ceremonial present *bo*) to wrap the gift from the bride's family to the members of the groom's;
   Pyebaekbo (bowing *bo*) used when the new couple offers ceremonial bows to themembers of the husband's family.

3. *Bojagi* used in Buddhist rites:
Majibo used to wrap the food offered to Buddha;
Gongyangbo used when providing elders with food;
Gyeongjeonbo (scripture *bo*) used to keep scriptures in.
4. *Bojagi* for special uses:
Myeongjeongbo used to cover the official recording of the deeds of the deceased during a funeral;
Yeongjeong bonganbo (portrait enshrining *bo*) used when enshrining the portrait of a deceased;
Giujebo (prayer-for-rain rite *bo*) used when

Sangbo.
Bojagi are ubiquitous and indispensable in the lives of Koreans.

praying to heaven for rain;

Jegibo (ceremonial dish *bo*) used to keep the dishes used during rites.

Bojagi can also be categorized according to their make-up, color, material, and design as well as the different classes of people who used them.

1. Different users:

     Minbo (folk *bo*) used by common people.

     Gungbo (palace *bo*) used within the confines of the royal palaces.

2. Make-up:

     Hotbo (single layer *bo*) made of a single sheet of cloth without inner lining;

     Gyeopbo (double layer *bo*) made with inner and outer sheets;

     Sombo (cotton *bo*) made with cotton inner

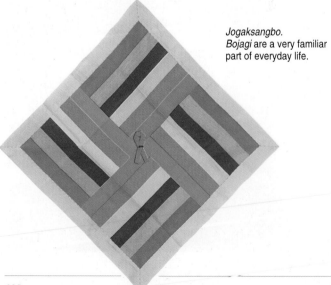

Jogaksangbo.
Bojagi are a very familiar part of everyday life.

lining;

Jogakbo (pieces *bo*) made by sewing small pieces of cloth together;

Sikjibo (oil paper *bo*) made partially or entirely of oiled paper;

Nubibo (quilted *bo*) made by quilting the materials.

3. Color.

Cheongbo (blue), *Hongbo* (red), *Cheonghongbo* (blue and red), *Osaekbo* (five colors), *Acheongbo* (dark blue), etc. depending on the color.

4. Material:

Sabo (silk *bo*) made of light and thin silk;

Myeongjubo made of particularly fine silk;

Hangnabo made of silk gauze;

Mosibo made of ramie fabric.

5. Design:

Hwamunbo, or flower figure *bo*;

Sumongmunbo, or plant-and-tree figure *bo*;

Yongmunbo, or dragon figure *bo*;

Unmunbo, or cloud figure *bo*.

In all of their diverse manifestations, *bojagi* have been ubiquitous and indispensable in the daily lives of Koreans. When a daughter was married off, the parents made sure that she took with her dozens of *bojagi* made with the utmost care and well-wishes. Through her and the generations of Korean women that went before and after her, *bojagi* use has flourished in Korea.

Korean *bojagi* continue to flourish with their versatility and myriad designs. *Myeongjujogakbo*.

Folk Paintings

Folk painting comprises the so-called "functional" pictures widely used by commoners in old Korea to decorate their home or to express their wishes for a long, happy life. Folk paintings, normally unsigned, often depict the same motifs as those of the so-called "orthodox" paintings including landscapes, flowers and birds, but abound with humor and simple and naive ideas about life and the world.

Ancient Korean folk paintings present the age-old customs of the Korean nation. Their repeated themes well represent the unique lifestyle of the Korean people, their dreams, wishes and artistic imagination. Though folk painting, typified by simple compositions of stylized motifs and bright primary colors, is usually considered a low form of art, it does not necessarily mean that all paintings in this genre are technically inferior to those categorized as standard painting.

Folk painting actually includes a wide variety of paintings ranging from those by high-caliber professional painters at the royal court to those by wandering monks and unknown amateur artists. Some pieces demonstrate marvelous artistry, but some are considerably less skilled

In ancient Korean folk paintings are portrayed the age-old customs of the Korean nation. A folk painting showing a Korean traditional wedding.

and sophisticated. The earliest examples of Korean folk painting, or minhwa, date from prehistoric times.

Picture and patterns in folk style are found in artifacts from all periods, including Neolithic rock carvings, early bronze articles, the murals and bricks in the tombs of the Goguryeo period (37 B.C-A.D.668), and handicraft objects from the Goryeo (918-1392) and the Joseon period (1392-1910). It may be said that folk painting has its roots in animal patterns on the primitive rock carvings, the four Taoist guardians and immortals in the tomb murals, pictures of the ten longevity symbols, hunting scenes and bricks ornamented with landscape designs.

Folk paintings were produced by artists who obviously belonged to a low social class in traditional Korea. But their paintings were used by people of all social strata, from the royal household and temples down to the farmers in remote villages. The paintings were needed for rites in various religious denominations like shamanism, Taoism, Buddhism and Confucianism, and for decoration of public facilities and private homes. They were intended mainly to stand for the common wishes of the

Motifs of folk paintings found in a tile from the Silla period (left).

The origins of Korean folk painting can also be found in the murals of Goguryeo (right).

public to repel evil spirits and to invoke good fortune, or to depict daily customs and moral concepts.

Consequently, folk paintings may be divided largely into two categories: religious paintings and nonreligious paintings. Religious paintings depict shamanist, Taoist and Buddhist themes as well as Confucian precepts for ancestor worship and moral discipline. Nonreligious paintings include genre pictures, portraits, illustrations of ancient episodes, documentary pictures, maps and astronomical charts. Folk paintings may be classified into the following categories by theme:

1. Tao-shamanist paintings

Longevity symbols : Pictures of the ten longevity symbols figure most prominently among folk paintings of this category. The ten longevity symbols, including the sun, clouds, mountains, water, bamboo, pine, crane, deer, turtle and the fungus of immortality, are often presented all together in a single picture. Also representing the predominant wishes for a long life are pictures of pine and crane, cranes or deer in large groups, and cranes and peaches presented with sea waves. It is of special note that the royal throne had a picture of the sun and the moon rising over a mountain of five peaks as a favorite backdrop.

Directional guardians and the 12 zodiacal symbols: Ancient folk paintings often depict the five directional spirits and the animal gods symbolizing the 12 zodiacal signs as an expression of the desire to disperse evil spirits and invoke happiness. The five directional spirits are the blue dragon of the west, the white tiger of the east, the red peacock of the south, the black turtle-snake of the north and the yellow emperor of the center. As time passed, the red peacock was substituted with a phoenix or a mythical animal called the kirin, and the black turtle-snake with a turtle. The 12 zodiacal signs are represented by the mouse, ox, tiger, rabbit, dragon, snake, horse, sheep, monkey, rooster, dog and pig.

Tiger : The tiger was among the most popular

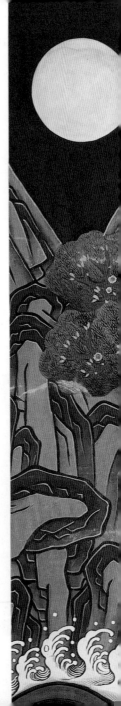

The royal throne had a picture of the sun and the moon rising over a mountain of five peaks as a backdrop, symbolizing longevity.

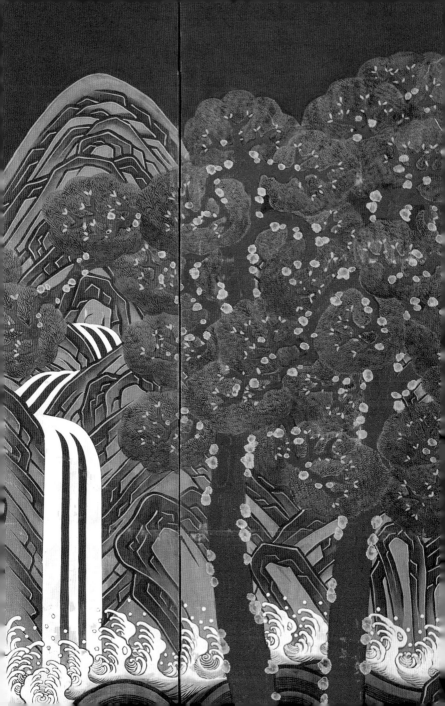

motif in Korean folk painting. Originating probably from the mythical "white tiger" as the guardian spirits of the east, the tiger was often personified in Korean folklore. A notable characteristic about the tiger as featured in Korean folk traditions is seldom portrayed as a ferocious beast but as a friendly animal, sometimes even funny and stupid. The tiger appears as a docile companion and messenger of the mountain spirit in many folk paintings. It often appears with a magpie on a pine tree, a

Immortals have been important motifs in the Korean folk tradition. Painting of immortals enjoying a game of go.

Magpie and tiger. The tiger was one of the favorite motifs in Korean folk painting (right).

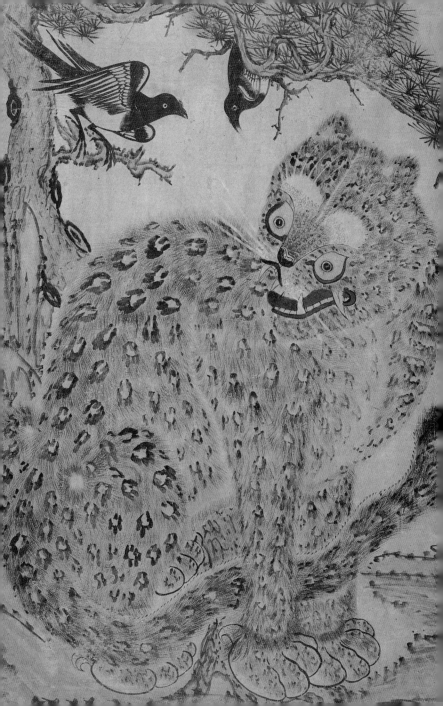

rooster or a lion. The magpie in Korean folkore is an auspicious bird believed to bring good news.

Immortals : As symbols of the Taoist ideal of harmony with nature as a way to achieve an eternal life, immortals have been important motifs in the Korean folk tradition over the centuries. Immortals, often portrayed as hermits in the mountains, were also believed to help the mortals to live happily, content with good health, wealth and many children.

The mountain spirit and dragon king : The popular mountain spirit and the dragon king motifs have their origins in two famous figures in Korean history, *Dangun* and *Munmu*. *Dangun* is the progenitor of the Korean people who is said to have turned into a mountain spirit in old age; *King Munmu* of the Silla Kingdom is said to have become the dragon king after death, and his remains were buried in the East Sea in accordance with his will. The mountain spirit is portrayed in folk paintings as a benevolent old man with a white beard, accompanied by a tiger messenger. The dragon king is usually depicted as a mighty animal flying amidst the clouds over the sea of high waves. The pictures of the mountain spirit and the dragon king motifs are housed at shrines in the mountains or by the sea as the guardians of peace and prosperity of the nation. Also appearing frequently in ancient folk paintings are various other Taoist or shamanistic deities as well as famous kings, generals, ministers or their wives.

2.Buddhist paintings

Buddhist temples and hermitages across the

A folk painting of a dragon believed to bring good luck.

country are rich archives of folk paintings, ranging from large icon images for ritual use to illustrations for sutras and anecdotes about famous monks and their portraits. These temple paintings are noted for simple compositions and bright colors.

3. Confucian paintings

Confucianism, based on the teachings of Confucius and other sages, has developed in Korea as an important intellectual and moral belief system. It also incorporated the nation's unique shaman and Taoist concepts of ancestor worship and respect of nature. Folk paintings in this category, included character designs of the popular themes of loyalty and filial piety,

A painting depicting the desire to enjoy long life with good health, affluence, and high social position.

pictures depicting the life stories of renowned scholars, and a carp jumping up from the river to transform into a dragon, symbolizing the widespread aspiration for distinguished academic achievement and a successful career in officialdom.

4. Decorative paintings

A great majority of ancient folk paintings handed down to the present were used for decorative purposes. These paintings generally repeat popular motifs with relatively poor techniques, but attest to the nation's religious tradition harmonizing various faiths such as shamanism, Taoism, Buddhism and

This character design can be classified as Confucian painting (left).

Confucianism. Ancient Korean folk paintings have the following characteristics: First, the folk paintings show an unequivocal yearning for happiness. They stand for the universal desire to chase away evil spirits and to enjoy a long life blessed with good health, materialistic affluence and high social position.

Second, folk paintings attest to the honesty and simplicity of the Korean people. The paintings are unrefined, sometimes even childish and crude. Yet they demonstrate the nature of the Korean people, prone to simplicity and unpretentiousness.

Third, the folk painting show the deep love of Korean for nature, humankind and the deities. They are full of humanity, peace and warmth of the heart, which can seldom be found in orthodox paintings.

Fourth, the folk paintings, with their bold compositions, dynamic brushwork and intense colors, display the indomitable will and courage of an agrarian society, oppression from the class and foreign invasions.

Fifth, the folk paintings abound with humor and satire. They manifest the considerable mental strength of the Korean people who are able to wisely surmount difficulties. Pains and sorrows are sublimated into joys and happiness with rich humor and satire.

Sixth, Korean folk paintings have a unique style which was derived from the indigenous artistic flair of the Korean people.

Korean folk paintings show an unequivocal yearning for happiness. This picture is based on the ten longevity symbols.

Sesi Customs

The expression "*sesi* customs" refer to ceremonial acts that are customarily repeated regularly during the year. *Sesi*, as days of festivity, act as a stimulus in life and accelerate the rhythm of the yearly life cycle so as to help one move on to the next cycle.

Sesi customs are based on the lunar calendar. The sun was not believed to show any seasonal characteristics; the moon, on the other hand, was believed to show these seasonal characteristics well through its wane and unity with the passage of time. As a result, it was easy to observe and appropriately evaluate the seasonal change based on its changes.

Farming, however, was based on the twenty-four *Jeolgi* or "turning points." In summary, *sesi* customs followed the phases of the moon, while farming followed the 24 solar terms.

The *sesi* customs tended to deal with *singwan* (view of god), *jusulseong* (nature of sorcery), *jeomboksok* (nature of fortune-telling), and *minsoknori* (folk games).

The gods included the *ilwolseongsin* (god of the sun, moon, and stars) in the sky, the *sancheonsin*

Sebae is a younger person's bowing to an older person as the first greeting in the New Year.

315

(god of the mountains and rivers), the *yong-wangsin* (the dragon king), the *seonangsin* (a tutelary deity), and the *gasin* (god of home). These gods were waited upon for they were believed to be able to manipulate a person's luck and fortune. The days of performing sacrificial rites are festive days, and people pray for the gods' protection and conquest of demons on these days.

Ways of praying for good fortune, which were also acts of praying for the safety of the populace as a whole, included "selling away the heat," "nut cracking"(nuts eaten on the 15th day of the First Moon to guard oneself against boils for a year), "chasing away mosquitoes," "treading on the bridge" (walking over a bridge under the first full moon of the year to ensure you will have strong legs and never be footsore), or "hanging a lucky rice scoop."

In an agricultural society such as Korea's, fortune-telling was performed to predict whether the forthcoming harvest would be good or bad, and depending on the prophecy, a good harvest was prayed for. Accordingly, in the first lunar month, when farming begins, fortune-telling was performed by listening for the sounds animals made and studying changes in the weather.

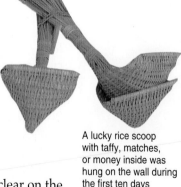

A lucky rice scoop with taffy, matches, or money inside was hung on the wall during the first ten days of the New Year.

If cows brayed or the weather was clear on the Lunar New Year's Day or on the 15th day of the First Moon, it was believed that a year of

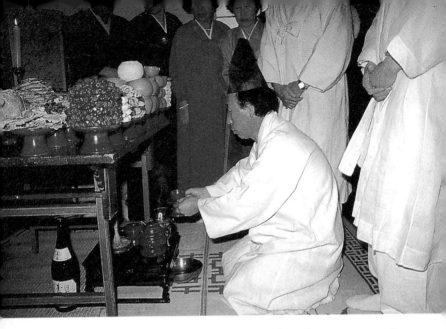

Most Korean families hold an ancestor memorial service on festive days, with items offered in sacrifice to the ancestral tablet.

abundance was ahead. When the sun was red, a drought was believed to be forthcoming. A northward wind meant a bad year, and the southward wind was believed to bring a year of abundance. In the case of folk games, whether a town's year would be good or bad was foretold via playing *yut* (a game using four wooden sticks) and a tug of war.

As a result, *sesi* customs could directly influence the policies of a nation, and at the same time, they were an important determinant factor in the character of the Korean people and the structure of their consciousness. Presently, however, with the influence of Western culture and changing lifestyles, *sesi* customs are vanishing.

During the First Moon, New Year's Day–the biggest holiday of the year–and the 15th day

were celebrated. On New Year's Day, Koreans enshrine their ancestral tablet and hold a *charye*. A *charye* is the holding of an ancestor memorial service on festive days, with food and wine offered in sacrifice to the ancestral tablet.

In the first lunar month, a fire was started on the banks around paddy fields to chase away rats.

Ordinarily ancestor memorial services were held for ancestors up to four generations back; for ancestors further back than the fourth generation, ancestor memorial services were held only once a year at their graves. *Sebae* (a formal bow of respect to one's elders) is a younger person's bowing to an older person as the first greeting in the new year. *Sebae* is done by kneeling down and bowing politely. After performing *sebae, seongmyo* was next. *Seongmyo* is a visit to the ancestal graves to bow and inform them of the new year. *Seongmyo* was a custom that was equal to doing *sebae* for living people; it was an absolutely necessary act of etiquette for descendants.

On New Year's Day and the first ten days of the first lunar month, there are various times when fortune is prayed for throughout the year. During the first ten days, each house bought a fortune mesh dipper and hung the dipper–with taffy, matches, or money in it–on the wall.

On the night before the 15th day of the First Moon, a straw effigy called a *jeung* was made and then thrown into a stream. This was to signify throwing away hapless fate and greeting a fortunate year. On the morning of the 15th day, drinking wine to "clear the ear" and cracking nuts were customs that were enjoyed.

By cracking and eating nuts with a hard shell (such as chestnuts, walnuts, pine nuts or ginko

Tojeongbigyeol foretells one's fortune for the year and was very popular among the common people.

nuts), it was believed that one would not suffer from ulcers. By drinking wine to clear the ear, it was believed that one would receive good things to hear; in other words, one would hear good news often during that year.

One of the most well-known *sesi* customs was treading on a bridge before and after the 15th. When crossing a bridge in the evening, one crossed a bridge the number of times equal to one's age; by doing so, it was believed that one could stay healthy and not suffer from leg pains throught the year.

In the first lunar month, families gathered around to play *yut* and hoped for continuing strong family ties.

One of the *sesi* customs that cannot go unmentioned is fortunetelling. It was customary to attempt to foretell one's fortune or how good or bad the harvest for the year would be. Particularly, *tojeongbigyeol* was very popular among the common people because of its monthly explanation of fortune and its high accuracy.

In the first lunar month, each town performed *dongje*. *Dongje* refers to a ritual ceremony that was performed as a unit by a town. *Sansinje* (a ritual service for the god of mountains), *byeolsinje* (a service for the special god), street ritual services, and a service for the dragon king are examples of *dongje*.

Ipchun, the onset of spring, usually comes in early February. *Ipchun* was believed to signal the beginning of the spring season. During this time, each house wrote a poem about the onset of the spring and pasted it on a pillar or on the front gate.

The first of the Second Moon was called

Children have fun kite flying, playing shuttlecock games, and many other folk games during festive days (right).

Yeongdeung Day. *Yeongdeung*, the goddess of the wind, was believed to bring her daughter and daughter-in-law. If it was windy, she was bringing her daughter; if it was rainy, she was bringing her daughter-in-law.

The 3rd day of the Third Moon was considered the day on which the swallows returned. As it became spring with its warming weather, people went out to the fields and ate a cake made in the shape of a flower. If sauce was made on this day, it was supposed to taste better; if a pumpkin was planted, many pumpkins would grow; and if any medicinal substances were taken, one was believed to live long without diseases.

The 8th day of the Fourth Moon is Buddha's birthday. It was also called Buddha's bathing day. On this day, people visited temples and prayed for the happiness of the dead while lighting lanterns.

Females washed their hair with iris and swung on a swing on the 5th day of the Fifth Moon, *Dano* (next page).

The 5th day of the Fifth Moon is *Dano*. On this day, women washed their hair with iris and swung on a swing, while men wrestled in traditional Korean style *ssireum*.

The 15th day of the Sixth Moon is called *Yudu*. On this day, people washed their hair in water that was flowing eastward, in the hope of eliminating bad happenings, and performed an ancestor memorial service with freshly harvested fruit and rice cakes.

Between the Sixth and Seventh Moons, there was the midsummer heat. During this period, people sought mineral water, enjoyed river fishing, and cooked very nutritious dishes, such as *samgyetang* (a type of chicken soup with ginseng in it).

The 7th day of the Seventh Moon is *Chilseok*, when *Gyeonu*(the Herdsman) and *Jingnyeo* (the Vega) were believed to meet each other on *Ojakgyo* bridge. On this day, people dried their clothes and books under the sunshine. Wives and children performed a sacrificial ceremony at the well (for abundance of water) and *chilseongje* (an ancestor memorial service for the Big Dipper God) to pray for the prosperity of their homes.

The 15th day of the Seventh Moon is called *Baekjung* or *Jungwon*. Various fruits and vegetables are abundant during this time. *Baekjung* means serving 100 different things on the table for a memorial service. On the farmland, a ceremonial feast was prepared for the laborers in recognition of their work so they took a day off for an enjoyable time.

The 15th day of the Eighth Moon is *Chuseok*, Thanksgiving Day. Along with New Year's Day, *Chuseok* (also called the Harvest Moon Festival)

is the biggest holiday in Korea. With freshly harvested grains and fruits, ancestor memorial services were performed, and visits to one's ancestors' graves are made. One of the dishes prepared for this day that cannot go unmentioned is *songpyeon* (rice cake). Inside *songpyeon*, freshly harvested sesame, beans, redbeans, chestnuts, or Chinese dates are stuffed. Then the *songpyeon* is steamed over of pine needles.

For *Chuseok*, *songpyeon* is made with freshly harvested grains.

On the night before *Chuseok*, all the family members sat around and made *songpyeon*, looking at the round moon. Particulary, single men and women tried their best to make *songpyeon* as pretty as possible. That was because one was believed to be able to meet a good-looking spouse only if one was able to make

Freshly harvested grains and fruits were used during ceremonies to honor one's ancestors. (left)

Ganggangsullae: Women gather to form a circle and dance under the full moon of *Chuseok*. (right)

good-looking *songpyeon*. During *Chuseok*, people share wine and food, besides playing various kinds of fun games. Games such as *so nori* (cow play), *geobuknori* (turtle play), *ganggangsullae* or *ganggangsuwollae* (a country circle dance), and *ssireum* (Korean wrestling) were performed, creating a lively atmosphere.

The 9th day of the Ninth Moon is *Jungyangjeol* or simply *junggu*. On *junggu*, people cooked pancakes with chrysanthemum leaves or made wine with mums. In groups, people went to the mountains or entered valleys to see the foliage, and enjoyed the day by eating food and drinking wine. Folks believed that beginning from *junggu*, mosquitoes would begin to vanish, swallows to fly south, and snakes and frogs to enter the ground for hibernation.

The Tenth Moon was called *Sangdal*, which means the moon shines the highest in the year. The moon during that month was considered sacred, and a ceremonial service was usually performed directed toward the sky. At home, people set the table with *sirutteok* (a steamed rice cake) to calm the household god for peace in the household, and replaced the gran jar of the tutelary spirit (of house sites) with newly harvested grain.

The Eleventh Moon was called *Dongjittal*; rice gruel (prepared with red beans mashed and strained) was made and served on the table which held ancestral tablets. The rice gruel was also thrown against the front gate and wall. This custom originated from trying to repel falsehood and was believed to keep away demons.

Dongji Bujeok:
To chase away demons, a *bujeok* (talisman) was attached to front doors or walls during *Dongji* (the Eleventh Moon), a time to end one year and prepare for the coming of a new one.

The last day (*Keumeum*) of the last month was called *Jeseok* or *Jeya*. It was a must for the people with debts to pay them off prior to the beginning of a new year. On this day, people caught birds, bowed in greeting to elders on that eve, performed *suse*, or cleaned the entire house. Bowing on that eve was intended to be a report to the elders that one had safely spent the year without any accident. For *suse* the house was lit by a lighted torch at various places to symbolically prevent the approach of minor demons.

Also, while housewives prepared food to treat the New Year's guests, men cleaned in and outside the house. In other words, they were getting rid of the past year's minor demons and misfortunes and were preparing to begin a new year with a pure spirit.

Additionally, if one slept on this night, it was believed that one's eyebrows would turn white; therefore, it was a custom that people would stay up all night. When a sleeping child was found, his or her eyebrows would be painted by someone with white powder; the next morning people would tease the child by saying that the color of his or her eyebrows' had changed into white.

Korea's *sesi* customs are part of old traditions rooted in life experiences. Therefore, *sesi* customs include an abundance of native wisdom.

Shamanism

S hamanism is a folk religion centered on a belief in good and evil spirits who can only be influenced by shamans. The shaman is a professional spiritual mediator who performs rites. *Mudang*, in Korean, usually refers to female shamans, while male shamans are called *baksu-mudang*.

When shamans dance, they enter a trance, and their souls depart their body for the realm of the spirits. By falling into ecstasy, the shaman communicates directly with the spirits and displays supernatural strength and knowledge as their mouthpiece. The shaman plays the role of an intermediary between human beings and the supernatural, speaking for the humans to deliver their wishes and for the spirits to reveal their will.

The extraordinary gifts of the shaman allows him or her to be naturally distinguished from others in society. The belief that the shaman communicates with the spirits gives that person authority. In ancient societies, probably from time of tribal states, the shaman assumed the role

When shamans dance, they communicate directly with the spirits and, in turn, the spirits, through the shaman, reveal their will.

of a leader as his or her supernatural powers contributed to the common interest of the community. As the possessor of transcendental abilities which were beyond the capacity of ordinary human beings, the shaman may be defined by the following characteristics:

First, the shaman has to have experienced the torture of the spirits by resisting being chosen for the vocation, which is manifested in the form of illness. The supernatural abilities of the shaman result from being the choice of the spirits. The illness breaks the resistance of the shaman candidate and the person has to accept the vocation.

Second, the shaman should be capable of officiating at rites in which they are believed to communicate with the spirits. The rites constitute an essential religious expression in shamanism.

Third, the shaman needs to be recognized as a religious leader with the ability to satisfy the spiritual requirements of the community.

Fourth, the shaman has to serve and assist specific spirits. This indicates that the shaman has experienced and accepted specific spirits at the stage of initiation.

A great variety of spirits are worshiped in the pantheon of shamans, such as the mountain spirit, the seven star spirit, the earth spirit and the dragon spirit. In addition to these spirits in nature, the shaman may also serve the spirits of renowned historic figures including kings, generals and ministers.

Shamans are divided largely into two types

A *baksumudang* performs a ritual to worship the *janggunsin* (a spirit of a general).

Shamanism is depicted in *Munyeodo*, a painting by Sin Yunbok, Joseon Dynasty.

according to their initiation process–those who are chosen by the spirits and those who inherit the vocation from their ancestors.

The shamans who are chosen by the spirits are endowed with supernatural powers to heal and to divine. They communicate with the spirits and speak for them in rites. The costumes used by these possessed shamans vary widely, reaching some 12 to 20 different kinds, representing the various spirits they embody. Percussion instruments are played in fast, exciting rhythms

to accompany the shaman as she or he falls into ecstasy by dancing.

Shamans of this type experience without fail the so-called *sinbyeong*, the illness resulting from resisting the call of the spirits, as an unavoidable process of initiation. The shaman candidate usually faints, has visions, and similar symptoms. Then, in a vision or a dream, the spirit who has Josen them appears and announces their being chosen, a call necessary for shamans to acquire their powers.

The illness will cause the future shaman to suffer for months, or perhaps for years. Statistics say that the illness lasts about eight years on the average, but in some cases, it may last as many as 30 years. In an extremely unstable psychological state bordering lunacy, the person can hardly eat and sometimes roams around in the fields and in the mountains. The illness, which defies modern medicine, disappears all of a sudden when the person finally gives way to the compulsion and becomes a shaman.

Then an initiation rite is held under the guidance of a senior shaman assuming the role of a godmother or a godfather. The novice shaman learns all the necessary skills of a professional shaman from the senior shaman before practising on his or her own. The apprenticeship lasts for about three years in most cases though it may vary depending on individual talent.

One of the spirits worshipped by shamans, *janggunsin*.

Those who become shamans by inheritance do not possess transcendental powers, and their role

is restricted mostly to the performance of rites. The rites they officiate at do not involve ecstasy for communion with the supernatural, and no specific spirits are worshiped. These shamans do not keep altars, and for each rite they set up a sacred passageway for the descending spirits. During a rite, the shaman does not embody the spirits but takes on a separate role.

The hereditary shamans use simple costumes of two or three kinds. But they use more colorful music, including not only percussion but also string and wind instruments as well. Both the music and the dance are much slower than those performed by the "possessed" shamans.

Rites are performed for various purposes in shamanism, a religious phenomenon with deep roots in folk traditions. The rituals are divided largely into those performed for the guardian

Percussion instruments are generally used during rites (left). Shamans use diverse tools during rituals; various swords to represent the authority of spirits, fans, flags in five colors, old coins or cases for bamboo fortune sticks, etc (right).

spirits of the house and the family, those for the tutelary spirits of the community and those for the deities of the universe.

First, the rites are performed frequently to invoke happiness. In ancient times, shaman rites were performed at all levels of society ranging from the royal household down to remote villages. Historical records say that the court of the Goryeo Dynasty set up 10 state shrines to perform rites to invoke peace and prosperity for the nation. Shamans danced and played music at these shrines for national well-being. Private rites were observed by aristocrats and commoners as well to pray for happiness in the family and in the village. These developed into communal rites and festivals in later years.

Second, shaman rites are purported to cure illness. Ancient people believed illness was caused by the spirits, which only the shamans could control. They even believed that the houses of the shamans were safe from the spirits causing illness, so, when epidemics spread, they took refuge at their houses.

When dangerous epidemics spread, the royal court invited shamans to perform rites to expel the evil spirits. At private homes, rites were performed frequently to chase away the smallpox spirit, called *mama* (lord) or *sonnim* (guest), both implying that it was an object of fear.

Third, shaman rites are performed to escort the soul of a dead person to heaven. Shaman rites in Korea are intended not only to appease the soul of a deceased person but also to unleash the baleful elements which brought about the death. This allows the soul of the victim to find peace in heaven and to never bring bad fortune to the living. Particularly, deaths from illness or accidents were considered to need the rites in order to guide the wandering and unhappy souls of the dead to heaven.

Shaman rites are classified into three kinds based on their style. The simplest form is offering prayers while rubbing one's palms. Rites of the possessed shamans are characterized by an ecstatic state in which the shaman is deified or embodies the spirits. Rites of the hereditary

Gangsinmu ("possessed" shaman) refers to a person who became a shaman because he or she was chosen by the spirits (above). *Seseummu* (hereditary shaman) is one who has inherited the vocation from their ancestors (below).

shamans also involve communion with the supernatural but the shaman and the spirits keep their separate identities.

In the shamanistic world view, human beings have both a body and a soul, or even several souls. The soul, which provides the vital force of life for the body, never perishes. After the body dies, the soul lives forever in the after world or is reborn in a new body

Shamanism classifies souls into those of living persons and those of dead persons. The souls of dead persons are personified, too. These souls are believed to be formless and invisible but omnipotent, floating around freely in the void with no barriers of time or space.

The shaman needs to serve and assist specific spirits. They are the spirits in nature and the spirits of renowned historic figures. A table prepared by a shaman for the *janggunsin* (previous page). Shamanist rituals involve experiences of ecstasy through dance. The influence of shamanism can be found in Korean modern dance (right).

Rites of Passage

An individual encounters many different stages in the course of life. A child grows up to become an adult, gets married, raises a family, becomes old, and after death is mourned by his/her offspring. In Korea, the stages that an individual goes through in life and the accompanying changes in his/her social status have significant meaning. The confusion that is likely to follow such changes is taken in stride through a series of rites of passage that are collectively called *Gwanhonsangje* (coming-of-age, marriage, funeral, ancestor worship).

In the Confucian society of traditional Korea, the coming-of-age rite signaled that the individual was officially a responsible member of society. Marriage reaffirmed the importance of the family as the basic unit of society. The funeral rites to mourn the passing of a family member and to overcome the resulting crisis in family life were austere and complex. The ancestral rite to pay homage to the family's forebears was aimed at strengthening unity and harmony among family members and relatives.

A Korean traditional wedding ceremony was held according to a set procedure.

The Confucian coming-of-age rite, transforming a child into an adult, was simple. For the boy, it consisted of tying his long hair into a topknot, and bestowing a *gat* (traditional cylindrical Korean hat made of horsehair) on the boy's head. The ceremony

A *gat* was placed on a boy's head when he reached twenty and became an adult.

was performed when he reached his twentieth birthday. For the girl, it involved rolling her braided hair into a chignon and fixing it with a long ornamental hairpin called a *binyeo* when she reached her fifteenth birthday.

Among commoners, the rite, as sponsored by the village *dure* (farming cooperative), tested the boy's physical strength by having him lift a designated rock. If the boy proved his strength, he was considered worthy of his mettle, and thus an adult.

Marriage in Korea was traditionally decided by the senior elders of the two families, and the ceremony was performed in accordance with

Binyeo was used for the first time to fix the girl's hair on her fifteenth birthday (above).
The Confucian coming-of-age rite signaled that the individual was officially a responsible member of society (right).

prescribed formalities: once a matchmaker confirmed the agreement to marriage by both families, the bridegroom's family sent to the bride's family a letter indicating the groom's *sajupalja* ("four pillars," indicating the year, month, day, and hour of his birth, which are presumed to determine his fate and fortune). The bride's family decided on a wedding date and notified the other side, which was followed by the groom's family sending the ceremonial wedding dress and gifts to the bride.

Unlike in China or Japan, the wedding ceremony in Korea is traditionally performed at the bride's home. It begins with the groom presenting a pair of wooden geese to the bride's family. The groom then exchanges bows with the bride, and shares with her a drink of wine in a gourd dipper. After the ceremony, the newlyweds usually spend two or three days with the bride's family (but the stay was known to last as long as a year in some cases). Upon arriving at the groom's house, the bride offers deep bows and gifts to the groom's parents and relatives, which symbolize the beginning of her new life with her in-laws.

Traditional marriage, modern style.

The traditional Korean wedding ceremony was an honoring of the ancestors and a public display that continuity in the family line was assured. The family, which was created by the marriage, was considered the basis of social life, and it was a social obligation of the partners to the marriage to lead prolific and prosperous lives.

Meanwhile, the funeral rites to mourn the loss of a loved one were played out in complex formalities and procedures in traditional Korea. During the Joseon period when Confucianism took root as the guiding moral and ethical system, funerals became particularly elaborate as an undertaking not limited to the immediate family but extended to the entire clan. Much of this tradition is still practiced today.

The purpose of a funeral service is to enable the bereaved family to overcome the sense of loss and fear and to smooth the transition to daily life without the deceased. The passing of one's parents is always particularly sad. For Koreans, the funeral–including the monetary contributions to the deceased family and the assigned duties and roles–symbolizes the full extent and nuances of the family bonds.

Traditionally, mourning lasted for two years, following a strict set of protocol involving a series of prayer rites interspersed over the period. The intervals between the prayers, including the offering of food to the deceased and rites to conclude the burial, would be lengthened over time until the end of the two years, the principal mourners would doff their ceremonial garb and other tokens of bereavement and return to their normal daily lives.

The various steps and rites that make up a complete funeral and period of mourning are as follows:

1. *Chojong* (initial departing):

Preparations are made for the hour of death and immediately thereafter. The family discusses such matters as invocation of the spirit of the deceased, dressing the corpse, assignment of roles and preparation of the casket. As death nears, a piece of cotton is placed on the nose of the dying body, to determine the moment breathing ceases. When the breathing stops, *gok,* the ceremonial wailing begins. The deceased is undressed, and the clothes are taken to the roof of the house, where the outer garment is waved toward the north, and the name of the deceased

The *manjang* (funeral ode) and flower *sangyeo* (funeral bier) lead the funeral procession.

is called out three times.

The garments are then collected in a basket and placed next to the spot where the tablets of the family's ancestors are kept. A curtain of folding screen is drawn around the deceased. The corpse is placed on a board with the head pointing south. The mouth is left open, and the feet are straightened and fixed to a wooden board. Meanwhile, a table of food is prepared for the messenger from the other world.

2. Seup (cleansing the corpse):

The corpse is washed and dressed. The fingernails and toenails are clipped, and the hair neatly combed. The loose strands of hair and nail clippings are kept in a small pouch. The undergarments go on first, followed by the socks.

Generally, the eldest son becomes the principal mourner.

Rice is fed into the mouth three times, along with three pieces each of money and beads. After the eyes are covered, the ears stuffed, and a band tied around the waist, the hands are wrapped and a sheet is placed over the corpse.

3. Soryeom (wrapping the corpse):

The day after *seup* is performed, the outer clothing and a cover with which to wrap the corpse is laid out. The upper garment goes on first, followed by the lower one. The other pieces are added on to form a square, which is followed by the final cover.

4. Daeryeom (placing the corpse in the coffin):

Before placing the corpse in the coffin, ash is sprinkled on the bottom of the coffin. A thin board with seven holes standing for the seven stars that make up the Big Dipper is put in place, followed by a mattress. The corpse is set in place, with empty space being filled with old clothing of the deceased. The coffin is shut and fixed with nodeless nails, and then covered with the final wrapping.

5. *Seongbok* (dressing oneself):

There is a set of procedures the immediate family and close relatives must follow in wearing their mourning clothing. It includes the duration for which the clothing must be worn: three years, one year, nine months, five months, or three months depending on one's relation to the deceased. The practice calls for up to the third cousins of the deceased to dress for mourning. Once everyone is dressed, the principal mourner, typically the eldest son of the deceased, offers a prayer to indicate that all have gathered.

6. *Josang* (visitors paying homage):

Visitors come to express their condolences to the bereaved family. At this time, when the principal mourner wails, the visitor is expected to do the same before the altar of the spirit of the deceased. He then bows twice before dismissing himself. An exchange of bows with the principal mourner completes the act of paying homage.

7. *Munsang* (hearing of death):

Sometimes the principal mourner is away when a death in the family occurs. If it is the death of a parent, he must first wail, change his clothes and start out on the trip home. During the journey, and when home finally appears in his sight, he may wail again. Upon arriving home, he bows twice before the deceased. After changing into his mourning garb, he wails again.

8. *Chijang* (preparing the grave site):

Once the grave site is determined, the hollow must be dug and the tablet prepared.

9. *Cheongu* (removing the corpse):

The corpse, which is carried to the ancestral shrine, is symbolically reported to the ancestors, and then brought back to the house and placed at the center of the open space.

10. *Barin* (starting of funeral procession):

The corpse is removed from the house and placed on the funeral bier. Before the procession starts, a ceremony is performed. When the bier passes by the home of a friend of the deceased, the friend is expected to stop the procession and offer a *noje* (street rite).

11. *Geummyo* (arrival at the grave site):

This refers to the process from the arrival of the procession at the grave site to the burial of the corpse.

12. *Bangok* (wailing upon return):

Upon returning home from the grave site with the tablet, the mourners wail again.

13. *Uje* (rites to console the deceased):

To comfort the spirit of the deceased, which may be wandering around aimlessly after the burial of the body, sacrificial rites are performed three times.

14. *Jolgok* (end of wailing):

The day after the third *Uje*, about 100 days after the death, a ceremony is performed to mark the formal end of wailing.

15. Buje (placing the tablet):

The tablet of the deceased is placed along with those of his/her ancestors.

16. Sosang (small service):

This memorial rite is held thirteen months after the death, to mark the first anniversary.

17. Daesang (large service):

This memorial rite is held twenty-five months after the death, to mark the second anniversary.

18. Damje:

This memorial rite is held two month after *Daesang*.

19. Gilje (good rite):

This memorial rite is held in the month following *Damje*.

At the grave, the casket is buried and the bier is burnt.

In addition to these elaborate funeral rites,

Koreans have handed down a rich tradition of ancestral memorial rites through numerous rituals that honor the spirits of their ancestors and seek their blessings for the living descendants. The rites provide a connection between the dead and the living. Unlike the people of the West, Koreans of old believed that the world after death is not entirely separate from the present world but exists on the same continuum. To worship one's ancestors, and to give them continuity in life through offspring was considered the primary responsibility of filial children. To this day, devout Confucianists offer services for their parents, grandparents, great-grandparents, and great-great-grandparents on the anniversaries of their deaths. In addition, the ancestors are offered a *darye* (tea rite) on the morning of folk holidays such as the Lunar New Year's Day. They are also offered a *sije* (time rite) at their grave sites. It is sometimes said that these rites breed clannishness and exclusivity; however, they also nurture intergenerational bonding and pride.

The *sije*, or ancestor memorial rite, is held at graves of five or more generations of ancestors.

Ssireum
Korean Wrestling

Ssireum, a Korean traditional form of wrestling, is a type of folk competition in which two players, holding on to a *satba* (a cloth-sash tied around the waist), try to use their strength and various techniques to wrestle each other down to the ground.

The history of *ssireum* began at the same time that communities began to form. In primitive societies, people unavoidably had to fight against wild beasts, not only for self-defense, but also for obtaining food. In addition, it was impossible for these communities to avoid coming in conflict with other groups of different blood ties. As a result, people ended up practicing different forms of fighting to protect themselves. During this period, when grappling was a predominant method of combat, various wrestling techniques were born.

With the advancement of human intelligence and political and economic development among local communities in Korea, *ssireum* developed into a military art. It can thus be said that *ssireum's* elevated status as a military art was a natural outcome of social development.

Ssireum is a form of Korean traditional wrestling.
Competitors try their skills during folk competitions.

357

By the beginning of the Goguryeo Kingdom (37 B.C.-A.D.668), *ssireum* was already established as a military art. This is substantiated by the murals in the *Gakjeochong* (Tomb of the Wrestlers), which is believed to have been constructed in the 4th century. Drawn on a stone wall in the main chamber was a vivid scene depicting *ssireum*. The mural contains a scene showing two men wrestling, with a referee judging the match. The location of the drawing implies that *ssireum* was a major part of Korean life during that period.

Ssireum's status continued into the Goryeo period (918-1392). A record in *Goryeosa* (History of Goryeo) states that in the mid-fourteenth century King Chunghye ordered soldiers to

Ssireum gained widespread popularity during the Joseon Dynasty. *Ssireum*, as depicted in a genre picture by Kim Hongdo. Late Joseon period. (right).

Ssireum as depicted on a mural from the Goguryeo period shows that *ssireum* was a part of ancient life.

compete in *ssireum* and observed the match during a banquet. It was during the Joseon Dynasty (1392-1910), however, that *ssireum* gained increasingly widespread popularity.

Evidence of this is depicted in the genre pictures of Kim Hongdo, which frequently featured scenes of *ssireum* competitions; it is clear that by the Joseon era *ssireum* had become well-known as a folk competition in addition to being a military art.

Virtually every country has seasonal folk celebrations that contain the unique characteristics of that country, and Korea is no exception in this regard. *Ssireum* contests, which could be held virtually anywhere or at anytime, were a frequent part of the various celebrations held throughout the year. Many *ssireum* competitions occurred during *Dano* (the May Festival), but also during other holidays as well. On holidays such as the 3rd day of the Third Moon, the 8th day of the Fourth Moon, Buddhist All Souls' Day, the 15th of the Seventh Moon or the Harvest Moon Festival during the Eighth Moon, townsfolk gathered to compete in *ssireum* matches as a way of sharing their joy and releasing mental and physical tensions from strenuous farming work that lasted from spring until fall.

The surrounding atmosphere became festive with the beginning of *ssireum* matches. On days when *ssireum* matches were held, gambling games such as *yut* (a four-stick game like parcheesi) and various card games, which were ordinarily prohibited, were allowed. Upon demonstration of a fine *ssireum* technique or announcement of the winner, the people would raise a shout of joy, and *nongaknori* (farmers' music and dance) was performed.

Ssireum is performed on a *ssireumpan*, which refers to the grounds where *ssireum* matches are held. While the rise of *ssireum* as a modern sport has meant that a *ssireumpan* is now prepared according to specific rules, there were no strict *ssireumpan* regulations in traditional folk

The winner was customarily awarded a bull, a symbol of strength.

competitions. A traditional *ssireumpan* was ordinarily prepared in a yard where many people could congregate, such as a large yard either outside a village entrance, where a zelkova tree could function as a pavilion, or inside the town. Preparation consisted simply of pouring sand in a circle over the *ssireum* ground. Posts were put up in four corners, and gold-colored strips were wrapped around the posts to prevent people from coming inside the ring. The reason for covering the *ssireumpan* with sand was to protect the wrestlers from injuries when they fell.

Ssireum practitioners were called *ssireumkkun*. Among *ssireumkkun*, there were quite a few professionals who toured around the country for *ssireum* matches, and the better competitors obtained nationwide fame. It was considered quite an honor to be a *ssireumkkun*, and the ability to compete with one's strength and ability in a *ssireum* match in the presence of congregated spectators was itself something to boast about.

The final winner of the *ssireum* tournament was customarily awarded a bull, which was not only a symbol of strength, but also a valuable asset in an agricultural society. Because

farming was primarily accomplished by a bull's strength at that time, it was a most meaningful and generous award in every respect.

In Korea today, *ssireum* has emerged as a sport in the limelight, rather than a mere traditional folk competition practiced only on holidays. Its popularity is such that matches are broadcast on television to enable people to watch from their homes.

Ssireum matches include group and individual matches. The competition schedule is determined by a drawing in the presence of the individual team's representative, while victory is determined by a player or a group's winning two out of three rounds of the match. Nonetheless, only one match determines a victory, depending on the circumstances of the match. The decision is made by the executive official after gathering opinions from the officials of the competition committee.

The *satba* has to be worn in a way such that a loop encircles the right leg and long waist strip is flexible enough not to be a hindrance during the

Ssireum uses various different techniques.
Some of them are shown in the pictures:
1. *ammureup chigi*
2. *apdari teulgi*
3. *ammureup dwijipgi*
4. *jaban dwijipgi*
5. *andari geolgi*

The grasping of the *satba* plays
an important role
in *ssireum*.

match. The juncture between the strip and the
loop has to be along the central line of the right
thigh. Prior to the match, the two players bow
toward each other and the judge's stage, then sit
down to grab the *satba*. Such etiquette stems
from respect for the ways of *ssireum*. The two
competitors kneel down on the floor, keeping a
ten to thirty centimeter distance between their
legs. They then lean their shoulder into each
other simultaneously and grasp the *satba*. At that
point, the player cannot step back with his right
leg. Also, the *satba* cannot be held at a point

beyond the mid-point of the right thigh or the waist. Upon completion of grasping the *satba*, the match begins with the signal of the referee.

When the *satba* is released by one of the players or a player is pushed outside the ring, a rematch is ordered. However, if one is pushed out intentionally or one hinders the opponent's holding the *satba*, a warning can be issued as a penalty. Two warnings become a citation; two citations result in the loss of a match; three citations result in the disqualification of a player. To enhance the player's spirit for the fight and to encourage him to perform his best, judging is determined by two wins out of three matches.

The time limit for the match differs according to category, which includes elementary, middle school, and high school and above (including college and general public). A match for the elementary and middle school categories is set for two minutes. If there is no winner, a two-minute extended round is held after one minute of rest. For matches in high school and higher categories, matches last for three minutes. If a winner is not decided, an extended match is held after a minute of rest.

Upon exhaustion of the second match time limit when the first match's winner has already been determined, the winner from the first match becomes the winner of the competition. If there is no winner during the first match, the winner from the second match wins. When the score after the first two rounds is 1-1 and a winner is not decided in the third round match due to expiration of the designated time limit, a player who has received a warning or citation loses the competition. If neither of the players has received a warning or citation, the lighter player becomes the winner.

During the match, a player who touches the ground with any part of the body above the knee or steps out of the ring is defeated. If a player purposefully pushes his opponent outside the ring or steps outside due to his own mistake, a warning is given. However, when the match is completed outside the ring as a result of a player's natural progression in a *ssireum* move, the player whose move determined the end of the match becomes the winner. Squeezing the neck, hitting with the head, twisting the arms, kicking with the foot, punching with a fist, covering the eyes, and other actions that hinder the opponent's performance become grounds for revocation of the right to further participate in the competition.

The judging panel consists of one chief referee and three sub-referees. In addition to judging the match, they are also responsible for administration of issues pertinent to match. The chief referee moves in and out of the ring and is expected to announce his judgments in a speedy and accurate fashion. Sub-referees are positioned outside the ring , one on the left and the other on the right. To ensure the fairness of the chief referee's decisions, sub-referees observe the match thoroughly. If an unfair judgment is announced or the chief referee is unable to make a decision upon completion of a match, they can request a revocation of the decision or a rematch.

The right combination of physical strength and advanced techniques is required in winning. The picture shows Lee Manki, the champion of the *cheonhajangsa*, the highest competition category in *ssireum* matches(right).

Sub-referees can also recommend the immediate cessation of the match when injury is likely to be incurred by a player due to the match itself or outside conditions.

When progression of a match becomes impossible because of an accident during the match, a winner is determined by an agreement made between the chief and sub-referees. Absolute respect for the referees' authority is expected from the athletes, and they cannot challenge any judgments announced by either the chief referee or one agreed upon by both the chief and sub-referees. When a challenge is raised by a sub-referee in regard to the chief referee's decision, or when judging by the chief referee alone becomes difficult, the sub-referee's opinions are incorporated into a final decision.

The chief referee announces the beginning and ending of a match or the decision of a victory using a whistle. If any situation arises during the match that is likely to cause a player's injury or the *satba* is not

held onto tightly, the chief referee may stop the match momentarily, signaling for the match to continue when the correction is made.

If a player does not appear in the ring after having been called three times by the chief referee, the player defaults the match. Any player who violates the regulations of the match, uses violence or violent words, or demonstrates any improper behavior during the match can be immediately ordered to stop such behavior or be withdrawn from the ring.

For effective resolution of the issues related to the match, a penalty committee implements the decision made by the judging panel in relation to any incident that occurred or upon request for suspensions by various committees. If any unqualified player is found to be participating in the match, the player and the group that the player is affiliated with are disqualified. All results attained by that particular individual and the group are nullified, and a suspension notice is given out according to regulations set forth by the penalty committee.

With the development of consistent rules and guidelines, *ssireum* has continued to progress from a traditional sport and self-defense method into a well-loved folk competition and popular modern sport that is a part of the lives of Koreans today.

Professional *ssireum* has become one of the most popular folk sports in Korea. Shown here is a modern *ssireumpan*.

Gardens

Korean gardens attempt to recreate the natural landscape with hills, streams and fields. They are usually small in scale, but strive towards an ideal harmony of nature and man. The principal idea is to blend the structures into nature with the least possible disturbance of the environment, because, in Korean mind, nature is already a perfect and an absolute entity that regenerates and sustains life.

In the long tradition of garden making in Korea, adding man-made elements to the purest of spaces is considered a violation and something to be approached with utmost care and reservation. The essential idea behind the Korean art of garden-building is to make it look more natural than nature itself. In many cases, what appears to be the work of nature turns out, at a closer look, to be the result of very conscious efforts. Korean gardens are characterized by a submission to nature in an attempt to attain beauty and function.

Korea has a long history of gardens. The oldest records date to the Three Kingdoms

Korea has developed a unique garden culture during its long history. This is *buyongjeong* located in *Changdeokgung* palace in Seoul.

period (57B.C.-A.D.668) when architecture showed notable development. An important early history of the Korean nation, *Samguksagi* (History of the Three Kingdoms) provides numerous pieces of evidence of royal palace gardens.

The earliest record of a garden in the book is attributed to the Goguryeo Kingdom (37B.C.-A.D.668). It says that in the sixth year of the regin of King Dong-myeong, the founder of Goguryeo, mysterious peacocks swarmed into the courtyard of the royal palace. In the second year (414) of reign of King Jangsu, the same source claims that curious birds flocked into the royal palace, another indication that the palace had a garden to attract such birds.

The book implies that Baekje (18B.C.-A.D.660) had gardens of higher aesthetical standards by saying that, during the reign of King Mu (r.600-641), a pond was made to the south of the royal palace with the source of water supply located 8km away. Willow trees were planted along all four banks of the pond, which had in the center a miniature island named after a legendary mountain in China where Taoist immortals were said to dwell. Remains of the pond are found today in Buyeo, the old capital of Baekje. It is called *Gungnamji*, or the Pond South of the Palace.

There is also the record that in 655, King Uija had the palace of the Crown Prince extensively renovated and a pavilion named *Manghaejeong*, or the Sea Watching Pavilion, built to the south

Gungnamji, located in Buyeo, the old capital of Baekje.

of his palace. The sea here is assumed to have meant the *Gungnamji* pond surrounded by willow trees, located to the south of the main palace.

In Silla (57B.C.-A.D.935), the founding monarch Bak Hyeokgeose built a palace in the capital city of Geumseong, which is today's Gyeongju, in 32 B.C., according to the *Samguksagi*. The book also says that, during the reign of King Cheomhae Isageum (r.247-267), a dragon appeared from a pond located to the east of the royal palace, and willow trees that lay to the south of the capical city rose by themselves.

The best preserved among all ancient palace gardens is *Anapji* pond in Gyeongju, which was

recently drained for an excavation and restoration. Built as part of the detached palace of the Crown Prince during the reign of King Munmu (r.661-681), the artificial pond had five buildings along its shore stretching 1,330 meters, each situated to command a full view of the pond. Of the five, three pavilion-like structures

Anapji, located in Gyeongju, the capital of Silla.

have been restored.

Anapji has curved embankments on the northern and eastern sides, somewhat resembling the shoreline of a river. The southern end is perfectly straight while the western side is angular. All of the four sides are lined with dressed stones. In the middle of the pond are three small islands alluding to Taoist sanctuaries.

In an entry dated A.D. 674, the *Samguksagi* records that "a pond was made with mountain-islands, flowering plants were grown, and rare birds and strange animals were raised in the palace." It is believed that plants such as orchids, peonies, lotus and azaleas, and birds and animals like swans, peacocks and deer were kept in the palace. On the shore and around the islands are simulated beaches made of rocks.

When *Anapji* was drained and excavated in 1975, many relics dating from the Unified Silla period (668-935) were found. They included a wooden frame which is believed to have been designed to grow lotus in a limited area in the pond. The entire floor of the pond was covered with pebbles to keep the water clear. On the whole, *Anapji* and the surrounding garden were designed in a microcosmic style to symbolize the dwellings of Taoist fairies. The entire area was so arranged as to create the effect of a landscape painting.

Another important Silla garden in Gyeongju is the one at the site of a detached

Fantastically shaped rocks were placed around the pavilion to give elegance to the garden (left).

One of the most famous gardens during the Unified Silla period was *Poseokjeong*, where poetry and music could always be heard.

palace in the southern valley of Mt. Namsan. At the site of its *Poseokjeong* pavilion, believed to have been built in the eighth century, is a water channel in which wine cups floated around during royal feasts. The channel defines an abalone-shaped area. The garden seems to have been a lovely sight with thick bamboo groves, beautiful streams and dense woods of pine and zelkova trees.

During Goryeo (918-1392), the pleasure-seeking King Uijong had various beautiful

pavilions constructed in a royal villa in 1157 as part of a project to build a simulated fairyland. He ordered one of the pavilions to be covered with fine celadon roof tiles, which was criticized as an excessive luxury by offcials.

The art of garden making in the Joseon period (1392-1910) is best exemplified by the *Huwon* garden of *Changdeokgung* palace in Seoul.

Stone materials are the most notable features in Korean-style gardens. *Ongnyucheon* at the *Huwon* garden in *Changdeokgung* palace (above).
Juhamnu of the *Huwon* garden where lotus flowers were planted in stone water holders (left).

Comprising some 300,000 square meters of the entire 405,636 square meters of the palace property, the garden is tastefully laid out with picturesque pavilions and halls, lotus ponds, fantastically shaped rocks, stone bridges, stairways, water troughs and springs scattered among dense woods, all essential elements of a traditional Korean-style garden.

Amisan Garden in the back of *Gyotaejeon*, once the royal bedchamber of *Gyeongbokgung* palace, provides another attractive example of Joseon palatial gardens. It has four brick chimneys adorned with beautiful patterns, stone water holders and fantastic rocks placed among the plants on the terraced flower beds.

Korean gardens allow visitors to enjoy nature as it is. *Soswaewon* at Damyang-gun in Jeollanam-do province (above).
Garden seen from *Hwallaejeong* pavilion at *Seongyojang* in Gangneung (right).

Not far from *Amisan* Garden, in the northern section of the palace, a two-story hexagonal pavilion named *Hyangwonjeong* stands in the middle of a lotus pond. A beautiful wooden bridge spans the pond to the pavilion.

In Damyang-gun, located in Korea's southwestern Jeollanam-do province, a woodland garden named *Soswaewon* (Garden of Pure Mind), built by a 16th century nobleman, offers a fine example of Joseon literati gardens combining Confucian idealism and Taoist naturalism. Approached by a long, arched gateway of a thick bamboo grove, the garden has a rapid stream burbling down a rocky valley by pavilions, a lotus pond and a water mill. It is adorned with a variety of trees and shrubs

including paulownias, plums, pines, maples, plantains, gingko trees, orchids, chrysanthemums and lotuses—all favorite plants among ancient Koreans for both their appearances and symbolic meanings. The idyllic atmosphere of the place inspired many writers and poets.

In Gangneung, Gangwon-do province, near the east coast, *Seongyojang*, or the Mansion of Ferry Bridge, maintains much of the stylishness of the Joseon upper-class home garden of the early 19th century. The mansion is comprised of the outer quarters for the men of the family, the inner quarters for women and children, and the servant quarters, each surrounded with low stone walls with little landscaping. There is a square lotus pond near the entrance, with a pavilion perched on the shore and a miniature mountain-island in the center, in a style reminiscent of a lotus pond in the Huwon garden in Seoul.

A lotus is one of the most important structures in Korean garden. *Hyangwonjeong.*